Life in Alaska

May Wynne in her twenties. (From the collection of
Dorothy Zimmerman.)

May Wynne Lamb

*

Life in Alaska

The Reminiscences of a Kansas Woman,

1916–1919

Edited by Dorothy Wynne Zimmerman

University of Nebraska Press

Lincoln & London

Chapters 13 and 15 have
previously been published as
" 'Settling in' in Alaska:
A Memoir, 1916–19,"
Pacific Historian 28
(Winter 1984): 30–41,
and are reprinted here
by permission.

The paper in this book meets
the minimum requirements
of American National Standard
for Information Sciences—
Permanence of Paper
for Printed Library Materials,
ANSI Z39.48–1984.
Library of Congress
Cataloging-in-Publication Data
Lamb, May Wynne, 1889–1975.
Life in Alaska.
Bibliography: p.
1. Lamb, May Wynne, 1889–1975—
Journeys—Alaska—Akiak.
2. Kuskokwim River Valley (Alaska)—
Description and travel.
3. Teachers—Alaska—Akiak—Biography.
4. Kuskokwim River Valley (Alaska)—
Social life and customs.
5. Eskimos—Alaska—Akiak—
Social life and customs.
I. Zimmerman, Dorothy Wynne, 1925–
II. Title.
CT275.L25292A3   1988
979.8'4   87-30023
ISBN 0-8032-2879-1 (alk. paper)
ISBN 0-8032-7927-2 (pbk.)

Second paperback printing: 1989

CONTENTS

*

ILLUSTRATIONS

*

ACKNOWLEDGMENTS

*

I have had considerable assistance in finding the background information and securing the photographs for this book. The staffs of the Bancroft Library, University of California, Berkeley, and the Huntington Library, San Marino, California, have both been exceedingly helpful. James Barker of Bethel, Alaska, a photographer, has generously provided photographs and information; and Margaret Felder Holland of Los Angeles, who was born in Akiak and went herself over the Yukon-Kuskokwim portage, has also been generous with information and pictures from her collection. I wish to thank Roma Rector, who typed the manuscript. And finally, I thank my cousin, Mary Wynne Holliday, and aunt, Mabel Wynne Ziegelasch, for their patient answers when plied with questions. Any mistakes that remain in the introduction and notes, are, of course, my own.

The route May Wynne took to Akiak.

INTRODUCTION

*

In the fall of 1916, May Wynne, a young woman from Kansas, traveled from Seattle to Akiak, Alaska, to teach in a United States government native school. She remained in Alaska until the spring of 1919 and later wrote an account of her years in the Eskimo village. Her story describes the difficult journey to Akiak (by steamer and riverboat and on foot), the ongoing life in the Eskimo village on the bank of the Kuskokwim River, and her own experiences first as a schoolteacher and later as a wife and mother during her early years in Alaska (she was later to return to Alaska for another ten years). There are few records written by women of the pre-aviation period, and most of those that exist fall into three or four categories. There is a literature contributed by Victorian lady travelers, who described their steamboat cruises along the Inside Passage, with occasional forays ashore. And there are narratives by missionaries, whose records are full of information but who were motivated, at least in part, by the desire to recruit more assistance for the conversion of the natives. There are also the accounts of a few hardy women prospectors who joined the great gold rushes. And there are, additionally, the records of a miscellaneous group of women including army wives who wrote letters and a few pioneer schoolteachers who braved the famed perils of life in the Far North on their own. May's narrative is in this last group; hers is the story of a woman who went to Alaska to teach and live. Although she went by herself, in her second year there she met and married a young American doctor; thus, her story relates the domestic experience, as well as the adventure, of living in an isolated and remote Alaska village in the early years of this century.

The region to which May adventured, the interior tundra of the Kuskokwim River, was particularly remote and difficult of access in 1916. The total population of Alaska in 1910 was 64,356 people, counting both natives and whites, and the Kuskokwim region was especially sparsely populated. Akiak had a population of about 150 people.[1] There was neither telephone nor telegraph. A news bulletin came once a month from Bethel, thirty miles down the river, in the winter, and mail was delivered by boat in the summer.

May Wynne was accustomed to frontier country, although to a less remote frontier than the tundra of the Kuskokwim. She had been born in 1889 on the family homestead in northwestern Kansas (Phillips County) to pioneers John Wynne and Mary Jones Wynne. John Wynne had left a farm near Abergele, Wales, at the age of twenty to take a homestead in the hills south of Long Island, Kansas. He then married Mary Jones, the daughter of two other Welsh immigrants who had settled in Mediapolis, Iowa. May was the second of eight children, two girls and six boys. She had grown up on the farm, learning to ride a horse, sew, preserve the garden produce, and cook. From her childhood she was known in her family as a "worldwide dreamer," one of those born travelers who are filled with feverish excitement at getting on a wagon, a train, or a boat and who expect marvelous revelations from encounters with the unknown (her experience in Alaska in her twenties remained the great adventure of her life). She attended the local schools and, after graduation, taught for a few years in various rural schools near her home, including one at a place named

Frog Pond. In 1910 she borrowed money to go to Ottawa University, in eastern Kansas, from which she graduated in 1914 with a teaching certificate. She first taught English in her hometown high school in Norton, but by the next year her "world-wide dreaming" had got her as far as a school on the coast of Oregon. From Oregon she went to Seattle during the summer of 1916 and thence, on impulse when the opportunity suddenly arose, to Alaska. Having reached the westernmost limit of the United States as it then was, she, like Huck Finn, lit out for the territory.

When May arrived in Akiak after her six-week journey, she found an Eskimo village on one side of the Kuskokwim River and a white settlement of miners, trappers, and traders on the other. The Eskimos of Akiak, like all those of the Kuskokwim and lower Yukon River area, were of the group called Kuskowagamiut.[2] Although their prehistory is obscure, archeological studies have shown that they were established in their villages on the Kuskokwim long before any European or American explorers appeared there. Of the two Alaskan Eskimo language groups, Inupik and Yupik, their language was a Yupik dialect.[3] Their food supply came predominantly from fishing, the abundant salmon of their waterways being the chief staple of their diet. They also hunted moose, bear, deer, and small game for food but were less dependent on game than were the seal-, walrus-, and caribou-hunting Eskimos who lived farther north.[4]

The first known visitor to the region to write a description of the people was a Russian, Lieutenant Lavrentiy Zagoskin, who traveled in the area from 1842 to 1844 on an inspection tour. He found that both the Russian traders there and the native people lived close to starvation at the end of long winters when supplies ran out, game was scarce, and there was no fishing until the spring thaw. The problem was more severe for the Kuskokwim Eskimos than for those farther north, who lived primarily by hunting.[5] Hunger at the end of long winters was a problem that Moravian missionaries found persisting even into this century. The Russian traders and officers were accompanied by Orthodox priests, who proselytized among the natives. The priests taught some Christian morality and ritual but generally did not remain to officiate and reinforce their religion. Nevertheless, Russian Orthodoxy took hold in some communities and has survived in Alaska.

After the American purchase of Alaska in 1867, there was still some fur trading in the Kuskokwim region, for the American Fur Company took over the assets left by the departing Russians, but the United States government did little to govern the Northland. Governance became a patchwork of bureaus and divisions, creating an inefficiency that continued long after Alaska was given territorial status and a legislature of its own in 1912. The next major outside influence after the departure of the Russians came with the arrival of missionaries of the Moravian church, a Protestant Christian group with headquarters in Bethlehem, Pennsylvania. They founded Bethel, about thirty miles downriver from Akiak, in 1885 and were fairly effective in spreading Christian doctrine in the villages along the river.

By the time May Wynne arrived in Akiak in 1916, the village, which had been singled out for special attention by the Moravians, had been almost completely Christianized. Edith and John Kilbuck, former Moravian missionaries, had been the teachers in the government school for native children.[6] Edith Kilbuck wrote a letter to a friend from Akiak in 1911, describing how she and her husband had persuaded the people to build themselves houses instead of living in their semi-underground traditional dwellings:

> From our first arrival in July we have talked "build houses" and now eight new houses grace the village. O, so much better than the old underground huts. A few houses had already been built. By another year there will

be no one living in the huts, but *all* will have houses. Some already have paper on their walls, *all* have coal oil lamps—and good stoves. The people are no longer what they were *years* ago when you and me first landed. . . . The people of the village are *all* Christians.—and only two families are Greek Catholics. The rest are Moravians.[7]

The Kilbucks also persuaded the people to raise gardens. Edith Kilbuck commented that "they have fenced in and dug up plots of ground, looking forward with great anticipation to digging 'turnips and not stumps' next year. The soil here should raise good gardens, as it is rich and fine."[8]

Thus, when May arrived in Akiak, it was no longer a typical river village. But in spite of the church, the houses, and the gardens, the basic traditional ways continued. The daily and seasonal life of the people remained tied to the old economy of fishing and hunting, and much of the ancient culture survived. May tells about the *kashgee*, or men's house, which continued to be, along with the church, a center of the community. Men spent their days there mending hunting traps and fishing gear; it was a guest house for native travelers; and the gift-giving ceremonies, although discouraged by the missionaries, were held there.

Across the river from the Eskimo village was a settlement of miners, trappers, and traders from various parts of the world. The Kuskokwim region had not shared in the great and famous gold rushes of the other parts of the Far North, but a gold strike at Canyon Creek, thirty-five miles south of Akiak in the mountains, had brought miners to the region. By 1916 there was a small community of traders, miners, trappers, and Lapp reindeer herders (brought in as part of a government program) on the south side of the river.

May had ample opportunity, then, as a resident of the Akiak Eskimo village for almost three years, to observe both the traditional life and the changes that occurred with the coming of the Americans. Her story of the life of the village is a record of a community at a point of transition. The literature of Alaska abounds in Sourdough Sagas of the Gold Rush Days—accounts of the beach at Nome, tales of the dangers of the trail, and barroom ballads. But the kind of "slice of life" story that May tells is rare, especially for the inaccessible interior Kuskokwim River country.

The records of the Moravian missionaries (largely un-published) are numerous and have provided invaluable information for historians.[9] May's approach differs from most of these accounts in that she is much less judgmental about the native way of life and expresses little inclination to banish the gift-giving ceremonies, as the missionaries and government officials tried to do, or to impose her ideas of morality. Nor does her record show her recoiling, as many visitors did, from the primitive conditions in which much of the native population lived. Perhaps, having grown up on a frontier herself, she understood that however "uncivilized" the Eskimos' circumstances, they had been able to survive for centuries and to develop a viable culture in their cold and difficult climate. Although May demonstrated an unusual and admirable acceptance of Eskimo ways and even learned from them—for example, how to weave a net for fishing—she still remained a woman of her time. She made friends mainly among the white residents on the other side of the river and apparently did not attempt to learn the Eskimos' language beyond acquiring a few useful words and phrases. Her vocabulary for local ways and artifacts is, for the most part, not that of the native people. In her narrative she uses the term *igloo* to describe any semi-underground dwelling, although the local word was *bar-abarra;* she calls the gift-giving ceremonies *potlatches,* although this was an Indian term; and she refers to the men's house as a *kashgee,* although the local word was *kazhzhy-yak.*[10] The term *Eskimo* itself, which is still in almost universal use, came from an Indian label meaning "eaters of flesh." The native word was *Inuit* or *Yuit,* meaning "the real people."

In many ways May conformed to the ideal of the "womanly woman" of her era and performed the part of the "civilizing schoolmarm" of legend. She quoted poetry (Longfellow), sewed, gardened, played the piano, and was skillful at teaching and taking care of children. These are attributes of the persona of her narrative, and they are talents she possessed in life. But May was not the dependent, housebound woman one might expect from these characteristics. She loved the outdoors and adventure, flouted danger, and eagerly sought the unknown. Like some of the educated, middle-class pioneers described by Sandra Myres in her book *Westering Women,* May had a romantic vision of the West.[11] She saw the wilderness as beautiful and marveled at "the Creator's handiwork so far in the North." She seems to have had little fear; although some of her experiences—like running out of food on the trail, nearly plunging through cracking ice, and anticipating shipwreck on the Bering Sea—would have made hair-raising sagas for Jack London, they seem to have left May undaunted.

Even going alone to Alaska took courage, for it went against the conventional wisdom of the day for a woman to travel and live alone in the "wilderness." Young women were expected to stay at home, and it was assumed that they would prefer to do so. May's contemporary, the poet Louise Bogan, wrote in 1920 that "women have no wilderness in them."[12] On the *Victoria,* going north, May's fellow passengers continually asked her—to her annoyance—why she was going to Alaska; and one tourist told her that she should be at home where she could "associate with decent women." As she says in her narrative, these were foolish questions, only showing the ignorance of the people who asked them. She felt they implied some disreputable motive or some failure at home. It was generally thought, she relates, that there were only three reasons people went to Alaska: "They went to dig for gold and become rich;

they were escaping the law and leaving a shadowy past; or they had been greatly disappointed in love. None of the above reasons were mine." When she first considered going to Alaska, she invoked the pious thought of wanting to be like her mother, "a guiding light," but in a native village rather than a prairie homestead. And there is no doubt that she believed she was doing good in teaching children to read and write English. But the reason she most often gave for her journey was that she wanted "adventure and travel with a chance to make money," and these seem to have been her real motives. She had always longed to travel, but she also had to earn her living. Teaching in Alaska provided an opportunity to do both.

The stereotypes of women who went to Alaska persist. In recent years, a prominent Alaska historian, after praising the "civilizing" influence of women in Alaska, went on to say that "like other frontiers, the Far North became the nesting place for fallen doves, shrikes seeking a mate, and officious mother hens."[13] These images of women who helped to settle the frontiers are being partially effaced by the publication of letters, diaries, and memoirs, both reprints and new discoveries, and by the writings of scholars who have studied the records of women who went west. In fact, the response to the wilderness varied with individual women as it did with individual men. Women went north as teachers, nurses, and wives, but they also went as prospectors, traders, and journalists. May is one more example of a western woman who lived an obscure but unconventional life. She, like many women of her era whose destinies are just now coming to light, had some wilderness in her.

May wrote her memoir of her early years in Alaska after coming "outside" in the early 1930s to live in Seattle, where she would be nearer her brothers and sister, who lived in the States. According to her sister, Mabel Wynne Ziegelasch, she probably wrote her memoir without the help of a journal or letters. But it is possible that she aided her memory with the

8

numerous letters she had written home from Akiak. She says in her narrative that she wrote every week, although of course the mail was not picked up every week. Some parts of her story simply contain more detail than memory could be expected to provide, but any letters or journals she might have had have disappeared. May wished to publish her story and attempted to do so, but publishers at that time were not interested in the reminiscences of schoolteachers, no matter where they taught. So May's manuscript languished unread for fifty years. She died in Palo Alto, California, in 1975, and after the death of her son, Frank, in 1981, the manuscript was given to me, her niece, the daughter of her older brother.

In preparing the manuscript for publication, I have done some light editing, eliminating, for example, a few redundancies and changing sentences that were not clear on a first reading; but I have left the text essentially as originally written. I have added notes to provide historical context and to explain terms that might otherwise be unclear. I have also changed the title; May called her manuscript "My Kuskokwim Heritage: Life and Loves in Alaska." I have changed this to the present title because the original did not seem sufficiently accurate and specific. The only inaccuracy May seems to have permitted herself in her story is in implying that she was a young girl when she went to Alaska—"a young girl just out of school." It is true that she was just out of college, but she did not go to college until she was twenty-one. Thus, she was closer to twenty-seven than to seventeen, more a young woman than a young girl. I do not know why she took a few years from her age, unless she thought the experiences of a very young woman would seem more romantic, more appealing to publishers and readers. Otherwise, in preparing the introduction, I have found her narrative corroborated at every turn.

CHAPTER I

Going to Alaska

Alaska loomed before me as the end of the world on the day
that I was engaged by the Bureau of Indian Affairs to teach in
the little village of Akiak on the banks of the beautiful Kuskokwim River, but it was a place that I learned to love in the years
to come. The new and irresistible opportunity to go to Alaska
happened very suddenly and unexpectedly. In the summer of
1916 I had traveled from Norton, Kansas, to Seattle, Washington, for a vacation in the cool climate of Puget Sound, and
was living at the YWCA on the corner of Seneca Street at Fifth
Avenue.

There I learned from a girl from Iowa that the Bureau of
Indian Affairs was hiring teachers and she had registered as a
teacher for the Alaska schools. She was eager to go to Alaska,
and soon the contagion entered my bloodstream. It would be
wonderful to go with her. My heart pounded with romantic
fever at the prospect, for the very name of Alaska was exciting.

While my friend was being interviewed, I sat in the reception room. Other people were milling around, going in and
out. All were strangers to me, but friendly. I found myself
talking with a sociable couple, a man and his wife from
Alaska. As the conversation advanced, we discovered that we
were from the same state and had much in common. They had
a home in the Chippewa Hills near Ottawa, Kansas, where I
had attended school. These people, Mr. and Mrs. John Kil-

buck, were in search of a teacher to go into the country with them.[1] Someone who could see the endless possibilities of doing good, both in and out of the schoolroom. A "good neighbor" kind of person—someone older than I, I thought.

But I was all ears and eyes! It was the moment to tell them about my own wish to go to Alaska. A chance to see the world. My mother's good red blood was in my veins, and if she could be a guiding light in a homestead on the prairies, I could do the same in a native village. But then I thought of the distance from home and my voice gave way. Before I could recover and regain my courage, my friend's conference was over; she was ready and waiting to go. I thought that was the end of it.

Later that evening when I was feeling depressed over having let opportunity pass, I was summoned to the telephone. A man with a deep voice spoke: "Is this Miss Wynne?"

"Yes, it is," I replied, rather morosely.

Then he continued, "Would you like to come to the Bureau of Indian Affairs for an interview tomorrow afternoon?"

All in a jitter, but happily, I answered, "Yes."

When the appointed hour arrived, I dashed to the office to see what was in the wind, too full of enthusiasm to be really sober. Mr. and Mrs. Kilbuck were waiting in the inner office. They both smiled as I entered and rose to greet me. "I am glad you came," she said. Then without any preliminaries, she asked, "Would you like to go to Alaska to teach school?"

Such a surprise! To be asked and not be obliged to ask. She beamingly added, "You will love it up there."

Little did I realize when I answered yes that that part of the country would one day be the most sacred spot in the world to me. "Alaska, my Alaska."

I later came to know Mr. and Mrs. Kilbuck very well and their friendship grew sweeter as long as they lived. Mr. Kilbuck was a tall, polished, good-looking, full-blooded Delaware Indian, a graduate of the Moravian school in Bethlehem, Pennsylvania. Endowed with a natural reserve, he weighed every word before he spoke. That day a gray business suit matched his graying hair. His dark eyes set in deep sockets under heavy, bushy eyebrows seemed to sparkle. His right arm had been amputated at the elbow, a tragedy resulting from blood poison caused by a stab from a hook while he was fishing through a hole in the ice. Only recently had he been appointed superintendent of schools in western Alaska.

Mrs. Kilbuck was also tall. Some people wondered if she had Indian blood in her veins. She didn't. She was a lovely lady of poise and balance, full of good humor, charm, and dignity. Her hair, black as her expressive black eyes, was brushed to a shine with not a lock awry. She was meticulously dressed in garments designed and made by her own ingenuity.

Mr. and Mrs. Kilbuck had gone to Alaska as a bride and groom in 1885—before I was born. They were living there when my geography pictured only ice and snow in that part of the world. They had served as teachers in Point Barrow, the most northern school in Alaska. She longingly said, "My dream is that one day we can return to that spot, where the ocean spray froze on the windowsill," and, she added, "hear again the wild ocean roar."

My eyes must have been wide in astonishment. One would surely freeze in that cold country.

I was really going to Alaska with them. All this presented new plans and problems. Money. More money to purchase warm clothing. But then, money was easy to get. Right at that moment, my brother Ben's trucks were hauling beets to the market in California. He never failed us when in need. All the Wynnes patronized him as their banker. He never asked the usual why and what for? A prize brother.

The time was short with many obstacles. While I was waiting for the necessary cash to arrive, I made a list of necessities and then priced the various articles on First Avenue, where the Alaska outfitters sold their wares. I was a bit nervous about asking the price and not buying, but the clerks entered into the spirit of my plans. No doubt they thought I should be at home with my mama.

On one of the visits to the hotel where the Kilbucks were staying, I met the young redheaded nurse who was going to Akiak and also the young doctor who was to have charge of the new government hospital there. He was unmarried and so was the nurse. They looked me over, but I soon got used to that. It was a comfortable feeling to make the acquaintance of those going to the same out-of-the-way place, especially since we were to live under the same roof.

Mr. Kilbuck was leaving in a very few days to look after business in the interior. Mrs. Kilbuck and I would follow on the next sailing. The hospital wasn't ready for occupancy, so the staff wouldn't depart until just in time to escape the freeze-up.

My money arrived, clothing was purchased, and my trunk packed in very short order. It was ready for delivery to the dock to be shipped directly to the Kuskokwim on a freighter by that same name. It was much too heavy to be carried across the Yukon portage—the way we were routed to travel. Now, at last, all loose ends were tied together and I was ready to sail, but for one thing—my last problem—to break the news to my parents. My mother wouldn't worry too much. She had always said, "Do as you please as long as the choice is honorable." But my father would object. How could I tell my father! If I wrote to him he would definitely tell me to come home. I couldn't go against his word, but now that all plans were made, I was bent on going, come "hell or high water."

After much worry, deliberation, and loss of sleep, I took the coward's way out. I wired my father just as the boat was sailing.

I called Mrs. Kilbuck to tell her that all was ready and I was waiting to go—the sooner the better. She didn't answer. That was strange. She didn't answer the next morning either, and in desperation I called the room clerk. She had been taken to the hospital for an emergency operation. She had already warmed and illuminated my life, but she didn't go into the country until spring.

I sailed with another lady.

CHAPTER 2

Ocean Voyage on the *Victoria*

In the middle of August 1916, I departed for the Territory of Alaska aboard the old steamship *Victoria,* a veteran liner that had challenged the high seas for almost half a century.[2] Her maiden voyage had been celebrated in crossing the Atlantic Ocean, where she served faithfully for many years. Later she was transferred to the Pacific, answering many ports of call in various sections of the Orient. Only recently in 1908 had she been drafted to the Alaska waters to carry both freight and passengers to the Northland.

This ocean liner had been bedecked with many layers of paint; even on this day of sailing she was being decorated by members of the crew. Paint smell pervaded the atmosphere. She had also been reconditioned with an entirely new keel, rendering her staunch and seaworthy after all these years of weathering the tempests, so she was not only good-looking, but also trustworthy.

The adventure of sailing on a ship was a dream fulfilled, and a big moment to a girl who had lived all her life inland with scarcely a hole deep enough for a swim. This was real drama in my life. Pure delight.

We stood in the long line to show our tickets to the purser; then we followed a porter as he rushed headlong up the gangway to deliver our baggage to our cabin. The wharf meanwhile was crowded with people coming and going; taxis were whisking in and out with last-minute passengers, and motor-driven vehicles were dashing here and there with freight yet to be loaded—all was excitement.

Three whistles sounded: the first was a signal that the liner would be leaving port in half an hour; in fifteen minutes more the second shrill whistle gave warning for all visitors aboard the ship to go ashore; then, in the last few seconds, the ropes were relinquished, the gangplank lifted, gongs clanged, and the bells from the engine room jingled as we slowly slipped from the dock—we were moving. There was a pleasant sensation as we churned the water and turned northward.

There was scarcely standing room on the pier. Amid the gay paper streamers of all colors, the passengers on the ship waved to those who had come to say good-bye to departing friends and loved ones. I was a stranger in a new and strange land, going to a new and stranger land with no one special to bid me a bon voyage. It took some courage, but my spirits were high with no self-pity.

We sailed in the early morning with the water serene and smooth. It was one of those sunshiny days in Seattle when all nature with its morning glow displayed a scene of splendor and loveliness. Puget Sound was astir with every description of seagoing vessel: there were tugboats, barges, fishing schooners, ferries loaded with commuters, a navy flotilla at anchor, palatial yachts, freighters loading for foreign ports, and ocean liners waiting to sail.

This interesting picture soon gave way to a panoramic view of all the surrounding country; the romantic outline of the Olympics loomed up in the distant west; very soon the long range of the Cascades of the east came into view; and to the south Mount Rainier, emblazoned in splendor, towered in the skies, like a giant ice-cream cone. That afternoon we sailed through the wide straits of Juan de Fuca, crossing the bar into the Pacific Ocean. This, my first view of the great blue ocean and whiff of the refreshing tang of the sea, was thrilling. The water seemed animated by a lively game of leapfrog as the breakers dashed upon the shore and then rolled back for another trial. The huge swells heaved the liner as they crashed against its sides, and those who were on deck were showered with salt sea spray. A horrible sickness took hold of me, and I almost wished I were back on land. Soon after crossing the bar, however, the sea was calm and peaceful, and my upset feeling cleared away. In a short time we were out into the open sea with the land out of sight.

To get from Seattle to Unimak Pass, the gateway to the Bering Sea, required seven days of continual sailing; but an ocean voyage is refreshing and restful; there are so many things of interest to be enjoyed on a boat. Some chatted and others read; many lounged lazily on the upper deck, perhaps waiting for a whale that might suddenly come to the surface of the ocean, shooting up its great stream of water like Old Faithful. The decks were never without someone promenading in the fresh air; then in the evening many passengers danced in the salon to the music of the ship's orchestra—music furnished by four Washington University girls. Others were happily engaged in their favorite game of cards. Fellow passengers on the steamer represented many of the states in the Union, but most of the number were seasoned Alaskans returning to their homes for the winter on this last sailing.

On the first evening I retired early to my stateroom. This was a comfortable, restful, and tranquil place to spend the evening with a pinup lamp and an interesting book to read; I could feel the vibration of the boat, hear the lapping of the water on the sides of the hull, and smell the invigorating fresh salt air.

Mrs. Corrine Call, the lady who shared the cabin with me, had spent years in the service of the Bureau of Indian Affairs and was now on her way to a new station, Russian Mission, on the lower Yukon. She, a motherly, cultured lady with beautiful gray hair, immediately took me under her wing; perhaps the head office had relegated to her the job of looking after me, since I was now alone, but I was rather proud of being her protégé. Her travels were extensive compared with my short excursions, and there was much to be gained from her vast store of experiences. She was born in Washington, D.C., attended the University of Chicago, and had journeyed as a girl to many parts of the world. A lass like me, who had been grounded on the plains of Kansas, had something new to learn about conventions on a steamer and life in general. For that reason, my mind often worked overtime, preserving all the added information about the new country that was to be my home.

This lady and her husband had served as teachers in a remote, isolated, and lonely outpost in the Bristol Bay region, a section of the world where mail was delivered only two or three times during the year.

One spring morning her husband went on a hunting trip with an Eskimo companion, Robert, to be away only part of the day. When evening came, neither of the men had returned, yet she wasn't concerned over the delay until the shadows deepened and the knowing stars were shining. Then something seemed to tell her that all was not well. She tried in vain to ward off the premonitions; she waited and waited, looked and looked, spending most of the night in suspense and apprehension.

At four o'clock in the morning Robert walked alone into the room and sat down; his very looks told of agony that he had suffered.

When she asked concerning her husband's welfare, he answered in a cold, matter-of-fact way: "Him dead. I carry him home. Him in woodshed."

She never knew what caused his death: it might have been

acute indigestion, poison berries, or a sudden heart attack, but he was stricken for some reason with a terrific headache, passing away almost instantly. She truly had her dark hour alone, and her experience was a foreshadowing of mine.

Mother Superior, Sister M. Amadieus of the Ursuline Sisters of Alaska, bound for the Catholic mission in St. Michael, was my first acquaintance among the passengers on the steamer. Dressed in her flowing black, she was an elderly, lovable, and saintly soul. Her keen wit and lively sense of humor were valuable assets in living happily in unison with other people, especially where one rubs elbows so closely in Alaska schools and missions.

She was greatly concerned over my future welfare and took an interest in my soul; she told me that a young unattached girl in that faraway land might, out of sheer loneliness, marry a man much older than herself. She was of the opinion that young men of my years were at a premium, since most of the men in that region had entered the country during the gold rush in 1898. Every day, because of her motherly instinct and interest in my behalf, she cautioned me not to do this and not to do that. Her worries at that time seemed to me imaginary, but I listened and learned anyway.

Had she known my father and mother, and the teachings they had instilled into my young life, she would have had no cause for uneasiness as to my downfall. My father had rocked me in his arms with his shepherd dog at his knee, singing his old Welsh songs: "The Ash Grove," "The Rising of the Lark," "All through the Night," and many others. He always called me his little lady, and now I was grown I would be a lady still.

My mother in her quiet way impressed us with the teachings of truth, honor, and virtuous living; we learned proverb after proverb with the essence of character building: "Nothing can need a lie." "Watch your Ms and Qs, modesty and quietness." "Keep your dignity and your own counsel."

Never could I disregard the training and discipline of my parents. They have now left this world, but their spirits are still my guiding star, and their memory a priceless heritage.

Captain O'Brien, the master of the ship, was a proud, broad-shouldered, red-faced Irishman, who piloted his steamer with pleasure in any weather, for he seemed to enjoy an occasional storm as well as the calm—his crew highly respected his command, but stood in awe, for law and order were carried out to the Nth degree.

This tall, handsome man was a great and interesting character who could make one's blood run cold relating experiences of his fifty seafaring years, but an outstanding characteristic was his superstition. Someone traveling on his ship had mysteriously hurled the black cat overboard. He was most enraged over this mean act, for the cat was his good luck mascot. The vessel was searched in every nook and corner, from deck to hold, fore and aft; they hunted among the steerage and first-class passengers, but to no avail—it was a serious affair with him. If the person who had perpetrated the crime could have been found, he too would have been hurled into the briny deep with no compunctions on the part of the captain, for he truly expected difficulty in reaching port after this act of bewitchery. It was, indeed, a stormy voyage on a wild, unruly sea, but his ship didn't founder.

One morning the captain asked me the name of my home state, and I answered rather proudly, "Kansas." He then told about a lady on the previous sailing. He had asked her the same question, but when she said "Kansas" she remarked in the same breath, "Now laugh." That wasn't funny as far as I was concerned, for I was proud of my home state with all its drawbacks; no grander people ever lived than John and Mary Wynne, my parents, and that was their home.

Our seven days of plowing the seas were coming to an end, for we were scheduled to reach Unimak Pass at midnight. All evening we had viewed from a distance the hazy, purple mountains on the Aleutian Islands. One was throwing off light and lava from its crater, but soon we went into the darkness, when nothing was visible save the black, rolling, restless ocean with the moon and stars looking down upon us.

It was almost midnight when we encountered rushing, swirling water and a pounding surf, with foghorns and sirens going full blast. The ship was stupendous in battling a powerful onslaught of water which rushed angrily through the narrows. It was lifted high by each furious charge of the mighty waves, which tossed it here and there; nevertheless, it withstood each raging attack and eventually emerged triumphant.

A lifeboat near our cabin had broken loose from its fastenings in the strong wind and was banging against the sides of the ship. I thought I heard the captain order it lowered into the water—my heart stood still—one might as well jump overboard as be adrift in a dory on that wild, unruly sea. But my fears were immediately allayed when a member of the crew calmly tied the loosened ropes and went serenely on his way.

This pass is a narrow channel with a powerful current; consequently, every precaution is taken to pilot the steamer through the straits in safety. This was a clear, cold night with millions of stars. Never did the lines by Longfellow have so much meaning for me as after our safe passage. "In the infinite meadows of heaven blossomed the lovely stars, the forget-me-nots of the angels."

The excitement was all over shortly after midnight when we entered the cold, blue waters of the Bering Sea. A stiff wind was blowing, and the boat was rocking more than it had at any time on its way. For that reason, I hurried back to my stateroom, expecting to sleep peacefully, but it was not to be. Before I could snatch off my clothes and crawl into my bunk, seasickness had taken hold—in a cruel way.

My bed was my refuge for the next three days until we reached Nome, and it was a miserable life—even in the bunk. The ship's nurse was much in demand, for only seasoned sailors could keep their balance. Terra firma was the only cure. The captain often made rounds to enquire about the health of the ailing.

My roommate, who seemed to possess an abundance of willpower, seldom missed a meal, but often she looked pale and distressed. She rarely failed to say, jokingly, "Aren't you going down to the dining room with me?" I didn't care at that time if I never saw food again.

One Sunday evening Mrs. Call told me in a rather stern voice, "I think that it is time for you to make the effort to go down to the dining room to dinner this evening; the lady in the next room who has been very sick is going, and she is much older." How could I go? I couldn't even stand on my feet to dress. But it was a challenge to my courage, and if she felt that way, perhaps it was better to make the attempt. I staggered down to the table for dinner, rather than be considered a weakling. When we were seated, the old lady sat across the table from me. In front of us was placed a beautiful birthday cake—it was September the third, her birthday and mine. Cut roses had been placed in our rooms while we were away— "Compliments from the Victoria's crew." This made it a happy birthday, even though we never tasted the cake.

When we at last reached Nome the weather was stormy with a heavy gale pounding the boat, and the huge, surging waves again swept overboard. Not even the lighters that usually came out to unload the ship dared risk the storm, so our steamer found shelter near Sledge Island, letting down anchor for three days.

Nome has never been able to establish docks that the waves didn't pound, wreck, and wash out to sea, even though millions have been spent in the futile attempt. As a result, the steamers are obliged to lie at anchor at least a mile from shore. Here they are met by lighters that take the passengers and cargo to the mainland; but in this way much of the freight is lost if the sea is rough.

My heart was set on going ashore to explore, but my chief had warned me before sailing not to leave the ship. If I did take the chance and didn't get back to the boat in the rough weather, I would be obliged to pay my own expenses for the winter—the very thing that my finances didn't warrant. I reluctantly remained on board.

From the ship, Nome presented a picture of loneliness, but we were too far out to see the town. The bleak, red-clay colored hills loomed up in the background, displaying a barren section of the world, but the people who live there appear to like it.

After we had been held up by the storm for several days, the wind died away, and the old ocean seemed tired and ceased its fight. Passengers and freight were finally discharged, and we set sail across Norton Sound for St. Michael, a distance of 128 miles. We crossed the channel in clear, cold weather with a quiet and tranquil sea; at this point we were to disembark for a lower Yukon craft. The first part of our journey was over.

CHAPTER 3

St. Michael and the *Sarah*

As we entered the port of St. Michael late that evening, we met a river steamer leaving for the upper Yukon. Missing the connection with this outgoing boat meant a delay of ten days before the next scheduled sailing upstream: naturally this occurrence caused much concern and excitement, especially among the passengers who were intent on reaching their destinations as quickly as possible. Indignant travelers hurried to the observation windows and decks to make sure that it was the Yukon steamer, the *Sarah*. Men swore, "It is purposely to give the hotel more business, since both are under the management of the company."[3] Actually, we had been unduly delayed by the rough weather, and they were only conjecturing.

Mrs. Call and I were not the least worried, and remained calm; the delay would give us time to explore this northern town and regain our equilibrium lost at sea.

It was late that evening when we saw the lights of St. Michael welcoming us into the village, and as in the Nome harbor, the boat anchored out a mile or so from the dock. Many of the passengers, ourselves included, remained on the steamer until morning.

When we signed for a room at the hotel the next morning, two young girls, who were en route to the interior, didn't

St. Michael, Alaska. May stayed at the hotel there
while waiting for the *Sarah*. (Courtesy of the Yugtarvik
Regional Museum, Bethel, Alaska.)

register; evidently they had hoped to find a less expensive place
to eat and sleep. After all, six dollars each day for ten days of
waiting was an added, unexpected expense. As we were going
to our rooms the hotel clerk was heard to say, "Two ladies
have registered, but there will be two more before night falls!"
He well knew that this hotel was the only place for them to find
lodging.

We were escorted to our rooms on the second floor, which
were most inviting. Though far removed from the States, this
rustic hotel, a large frame building overlooking Norton Sound,
was a lovely place to rest and wait for the next installment of
our journey; the food, too, was delicious. Perhaps our appetites were whetted by the change of climate—we were always hungry.

The room steward left without giving us a key. I took it for
granted that he had forgotten and was going to the office to ask

for one. Mrs. Call quickly dissuaded me, saying, "Oh, you can't do that. Doors are never locked in Alaska." Then, to be sure I wouldn't ask, she continued, "You would only offend the management by asking for a key." This was a new experience—no key.

That evening Mrs. Call and I pushed and pulled and struggled with the heavy mahogany dresser until we had it across the door as a barricade. I dared to say, "Asking for a key would be a much easier way of locking yourself in your room and save wrecking the furniture." And furthermore, "Why go to so much trouble?" She said, "The doors are very close together, and someone could mistake mine for some neighbor's. It is merely for protection." By that time, she had me frightened to the extent that I asked to sleep with her. Instead she came into my room through the connecting doors and we both tussled with my bureau, which was much larger and heavier than hers, until it was safely across my door. "Now you can sleep in peace and comfort with the air blowing from Norton Sound," she said.

We retired early that night, tired from long walks throughout the day, but sleep wasn't in my soul. Loneliness for my home had taken hold of me. The September moon riding high, the water lapping on the shore, and the lonely, whistling wind helped to lower the degree of my happiness. I could hear voices, rough conversation and swearing, from the adjoining room. A foursome evidently were playing a game of cards. They didn't disturb me then, but I was suddenly awakened in the small hours of the night when a woman's voice cried out, "Ouch, damn you, stop it." Unable to go back to sleep, I went to the next room to spend the rest of the night with Mrs. Call where I felt more secure.

The next morning as we were coming down the stairway, my name was heard, "Calling Miss Wynne, please." That was the first time that I had ever been paged; at first it gave me a feeling of importance, but immediately my self-esteem turned to fear and anxiety as a yellow slip was handed to me by the office clerk.

My first thought was "Perhaps the telegram is from my father in answer to my message." My flesh turned to goose pimples and a chill ran up my spine. In those days in our family telegrams usually signified bad news, so the message was fearfully opened.

It wasn't bad news, yet it wasn't good. The dispatch was from the headquarters in Seattle. The freighter carrying my possessions had been wrecked on the rocks, and my baggage, though safe, wouldn't arrive until the spring navigation.

Here I was, practically without a change of clothing. They suggested that purchases be made in St. Michael to tide me over until my trunk could be sent to the country. We had been permitted to sail with only hand luggage that we ourselves could carry across the Yukon portage, which was, indeed, very little and scarcely sufficient to keep me trim for the winter. My trunk had been packed with woolen blankets, warm clothing, including mittens and long underwear, felt shoes, and all the necessities, with few luxuries. Now my worries really began, for my purse contained fifty dollars; to ration that small amount over so many needs was a sobering problem.

That morning after breakfast we went on a shopping tour, visiting two or three different stores to compare prices before buying. Men in Alaska usually spend part of their money with each trader, thereby showing no partiality to any one merchant; but my small pittance wouldn't make or break any storekeeper. Finally, in one shop everything essential was available. When these purchases were paid for, I was left with only ten dollars, which had to be saved for necessities during the rest of the trip.

It made me uneasy to be so short of money. How could I survive on ten dollars until I received my first month's salary? Perhaps it would have been wiser to remain in the States, I thought, but now it was too late to reconsider. My parents had told me never to borrow money from a friend, for banks were in operation for that purpose. Here I was, a stranger among newfound friends, and there was no bank to even ask if they would trust me. I was told that "Alaska is the best place in the world to be broke, for when the tide is out the table is set." Any store would have gladly granted me credit, but my false pride kept me from asking for help.

Now, in spite of my personal worries, we went on a tour of the town, on foot, of course, but the landmarks were few. The old wooden blockhouse to ward off the Yukon Indians stood as a reminder of the Russian occupation; it was a many-sided structure with bullet holes sprinkled in its walls as a result of target practice and merrymaking. A rusty old gun was all that it contained now. Yet within its walls lurked stories of other days.

The citizens of the town were few: the town marshal, traders and their families, missionaries, schoolteachers, and the native people. During the summer months, members of the steamship company and their wives and children were temporary residents.

Boardwalks led out for a long distance to the wireless station, then to the fort of St. Michael, and from there back to the village, forming a triangle. This boardwalk covered oozing tundra moss in the summer and saved the stroller from sinking into the soft mud. It furnished a splendid promenade for out-of-door diversion, and we made good use of it every day of our stay. It was a good feeling to be on land once more.

The cold winds sweeping across the waters of Norton Bay chilled me to the bone. Could I survive the cold, frigid winter in the North? But . . . others did, so why shouldn't I?

While we were in St. Michael we made a daily visit up the hill to chat with Mother Superior and on Sunday worshiped in her church. In this same church we again met Captain O'Brien of the *Victoria,* who never missed Mass when in port. He walked proudly, dressed in his blue civilian suit, carrying a gold-headed cane. I never saw him alive after that day, but years later attended his funeral in Seattle, when he died in his eightieth year.

After ten days of leisurely, lazy living we said good-bye to the *Victoria* and boarded the steamer, *Sarah,* for the Yukon River. We were much relieved, as it was growing colder with signs of fall in the air; besides, we had the most tedious portion of our journey ahead and we must be at our posts before the ice came.

The steamer, *Sarah,* wasn't nearly as large and luxurious as the liner *Victoria,* but it was very clean and comfortable. There would be no seasickness to be endured, which more than offset any lack of splendor; still, it was a bit rough as we sailed out into the Bering Sea to enter the Yukon River.

The estuary of this river, which branches out into a fanlike delta, has so many channels that only a seasoned pilot knows which course to follow. Each slough seems to a stranger to be exactly like all the rest, but the navigators have their landmarks and know which one to enter. Nature has been persistently dredging through the years, working like a bulldozer to pour mud and silt into the Bering Sea, yet the pilots find their way in daylight or darkness.

River travel was quite different from sea travel. On the ocean we couldn't stop to refuel, but here we anchored along the riverbank to load on wood by the cords to keep the power up and the steamer moving. For three days we looked upon the mud flats, and only when Captain Lancaster invited us to the pilothouse could we see beyond the banks and over the rolling, barren tundra.

Occasionally the boat stopped for our pleasure to visit the graveyard of the once-splendid old steamers now consigned to the scrap heap. We were greatly amazed at the beauty of these palatial craft left to rot and decay, but they had served their time during the days of the gold rush. Most of these relics of the past had been decorated throughout by hand-painted door panels; but now these were missing, either through salvage by the owners or pilfering by souvenir hunters. We docked at a village, now and then, either to discharge cargo or to take on freight. Here, too, some passengers left the ship, but others came on board, so that faces changed from old to new as we surely and slowly moved up the river.

One whole day was spent up the Andreafsky River, a fresh-water stream made famous by the Russians. Here they had erected a fort for protection against the Yukon Indians, and it was the first fresh water sighted from the Bering Sea where they could service their boats after entering the mouth of the river. Our docking on the banks was for the sole purpose of overhauling the engines and removing the barnacles from the surface of the boat. We had expected this stop to be quite tedious, but we found much that was interesting, and time was not the least monotonous.

While the crew worked on the steamer, the few passengers climbed ashore to hike over the hillside, pick berries, and explore. We hadn't gone far on this ramble when we sighted the abandoned winter quarters of the Northern Commercial Company—a ghost of a place at that time. We wandered from room to room in the large rustic hotel and gave the shops a quick once-over before departing; it was a forlorn and desolate place, as the wind whistled through the deserted rooms. We picked our fill of berries; water gurgled in our shoes from the soft mud of the tundra.

Members of the company in earlier days were obliged to serve their turn in this remote camp as caretakers and to be on hand to service the boats when navigation opened in the spring. Our Captain Lancaster and his wife had spent a winter in this hibernation. He said that being a shut-in was wearing on the nerves, and consequently, when the long season ended, many were not on speaking terms; but happily, as the ice melted and left the river, grievances, likewise, vanished with the ice.

In the morning of our fifth day of river life we docked at Russian Mission, where we were to part with all but two of our fellow passengers. Mrs. Call, teacher, companion, and good friend during the entire journey from Seattle, was to remain here, for this was her new teaching post. Two girls and I still had the portage ahead of us. There was no hotel for ladies at this junction, but Mrs. Call invited me along with the other girls to share her home.

This house was a spacious building, having been built over the same plan as most of the government schoolhouses, and it was completely furnished, save a few personal touches that the occupant might add. The first floor of the house included a large living room and a combined kitchen and dining room; then on the second floor were two roomy bedrooms with ample closet space. An ell was attached to this section for the school, so that both home and school were under the same roof. The building hugged the hillside with a view of the mighty Yukon and the surrounding country.

We had learned something of the Eskimo life in St. Michael, but this was the first real initiation to the fur-clad natives, odors of seal oil, and chained malamute dogs howling from the tops of their doghouses. All the inhabitants of this little colony were natives except the Russian who had charge of the Catholic church, the schoolteacher, and the trader, but this trader had gone partly native in his habits and ways of living.

Three days were whiled away in this little once-Russian village as we waited for the preparations for the last lap of our pilgrimage. We were reluctant to leave Mrs. Call alone, but she was most capable and happy to be there.

At Russian Mission we had expected to make connections with the mail carrier, Oscar Samuelson,[4] who had transported the mail winter and summer from the Yukon to the Kuskokwim for nearly twenty years; but to our dismay, he had departed the day before our arrival. Traveling with this old-timer would have been comparable to a first-class passage

31

without the risk of losing the trail. But luckily, Mr. Kilbuck, who had preceded me from Seattle, had just come down the river and was in the vicinity, so we were going over the portage with him. He was the possessor of two canoes, one of which he had purchased for our special benefit; besides, he had carried with him an Evinrude from the States to be used in his many travels up and down the Kuskokwim River. As a result, we were well equipped for the days of travel ahead. Then, too, he had engaged an Eskimo guide who knew every bend in the rivers and the trails across the land to warrant us a safe passage.[5]

CHAPTER 4

Portage from the Yukon River to the Kuskokwim

There were six in our party, all of varied interest, and by heritage from different parts of the world: an Eskimo, a Norwegian youth, a Norwegian girl, a Scotch lass, an Indian, and a Welsh girl. Our leader and manager of the remaining trek was Mr. Kilbuck. He struck me again as he had in Seattle: as an extraordinary character, a stalwart man with a clear, straightforward profile and a face engraved with lines of character from years of service and experience; though weather-beaten from the cold and wind, it expressed happiness and warmth. He was very quiet and reserved with an air of dignity, possessing many of the attributes of his race; he loved the out-of-doors. If he was your friend, he was loyal to the last.

The young man, Ole Andersen, a miner, was a tall, fair-complexioned Norwegian, with all the earmarks of his country in looks and speech: sun-bleached hair, blue, stern, piercing eyes, and a bright, handsome face; his outdoor life had given him a mighty chest and shoulders. We were fortunate to travel with this youth, for the previous year he and his older brother had made the long trek with snowshoes over the trail from Valdez to Akiak. He knew the ruggedness of the country and how to cope with each new situation. He gathered tundra grass and taught us how to make soles for our mukluks, carried everything to the boats when the water was deep, chopped the wood, and did everything possible to ease the journey. Besides all this, he was the most even-tempered man I have ever known.

Ole had just traveled over the portage from the Kuskokwim to meet his bride-to-be, from Hammerfest, Norway, but after all his anticipated joy she wasn't there; instead, he received a wire saying that she wouldn't arrive until spring. Her sister had died soon after she had embarked for America, and she had left the steamer to return to her home. There would be a long wait for both until the next year.

The two girls in our party, Elizabeth Windberg and Ruby Russel, were young, carefree, and unconventional, full of enthusiasm and activity, brides-to-be when the journey ended. Elizabeth was from Michigan, a brunette with beautiful dark blue eyes, a pretty face, sturdy body, and the will to work. She was from a farm, boasted that she could milk a cow and pitch hay, and was the only girl that could wield the oars in a strong current. At times when the going was hard, she would sing, "I wish I were in Michigan again, down on the farm." Ruby was the opposite in looks and disposition, a city girl from Utah, too much out of her sphere to be really happy in the North. She had been on the stage and needed people rather than a quiet life in a beautiful country. En route to marry a good-looking trader, whom she had met on one of his buying trips on the outside, she found setbacks most trying and monotonous; nevertheless, she generally possessed the qualities of gameness and sportsmanship.

Our guide was a lean, lank middle-aged Eskimo, whose first name was Peter. He was a native of Russian Mission, and knowing the land and every bend in the river, he was the official guide for travelers going from the Yukon to the Kuskokwim. He smiled at us and said, "Me takum pay. Me no gettum lost."

I was sixth of these wanderers. The lure of adventure and

travel with a chance to make money were my reasons for coming to this vast territory. We don't see ourselves as others see us, but picture a girl just out of school with brown eyes and dark hair combed in a figure eight on the back of her head, and you have at least a partial sketch of me.

I was often asked the question, "Why are you going to the interior of Alaska?" There was nothing strange about it, as far as I could see. I was hired by the United States government to teach school. The next day some other person out of curiosity would ask, "Why are you going so far away?" They seemed to think I must belong to one of three categories, and they would like to know definitely which one, for it was generally assumed that a person entered Alaska for one of three reasons. They went to dig for gold and become rich; they were escaping the law and leaving a shadowy past; or they had been greatly disappointed in love. None of the above reasons were mine. I needed money to continue my education and would gain it through patience and perseverance in the schoolroom.

We sailed out of Russian Mission on a glorious afternoon with the six of us in our entourage. It was a good feeling to be moving again as we headed down the river to the slough with two small boats, one of which was equipped with an Evinrude; the other, a canoe, was towed in the rear. Peter, the Eskimo guide, proudly preceded us in his lively little kayak.

When we started down the river, the engine for some reason refused to budge. It was evident that the owner of the motor, Mr. Kilbuck, was neither a mechanic nor an engineer, though we gave him the benefit of the doubt since he was a man with one arm. Then, too, Evinrudes are a capricious piece of mechanism; they must be coaxed and coaxed interminably before they will ignite the gasoline. Sometimes it seems hopeless— then again they start off with a bang. A can of ether might have put the motor in action, but we had no ether.

There was little concern that afternoon when the Evinrude balked, for we drifted easily down the stream with the current while our eyes devoured the beauty encircling us. The sparkling water, as it glistened in the sunlight, was a pleasing contrast to the muddy Yukon flats. From time to time a fish could be seen darting above the rippling eddies. It was a distance of ten miles downstream before we reached the slough, which led upstream to the portage.

Drifting with the river had been an easy, lazy way of going, but here we were confronted with the toilsome task of opposing the current. Our "lily-white" hands were soon blistered and our unused muscles ached from the unexpected work of rowing, but we kept moving in a snaillike fashion. I had enjoyed my rowing experience on a gentle stream, the Marais des Cygnes, in Kansas as a coed on a beautiful moonlit night, but there wasn't the least bit of romance in this task. The onslaught of water charging us required us to use all our strength and skill to progress even slowly. Our guide kept on going ahead of us as if he were in a gala parade, while we took turns rowing as the motor was being overhauled. But it appeared to have no interest in life; it wouldn't even spark.

We hadn't covered the required quota of miles that day when the shadows began to lengthen. We should have traveled until dark, but we were hungry, tired, and lacked enthusiasm; so with all concurring, we made camp for the night.

There were no Girl Scouts in my hometown, but I wondered how it had been possible to escape the joy of camping out for at least one night. Erecting the tent like our Indian friends was a thrill—though perhaps we were more a hindrance than a help. The men raised the frame while we fastened the cover, tugging and stretching until it was securely tied to the pegs that were driven into the ground. It would not have been pleasant to have a gust of wind whip the canvas shelter from over our heads as we slept; and just to tease us someone said, "A wild animal might poke his head into our tent tonight." It was important to have the tent well secured to keep out the cold and also high enough to move around in with ease as we prepared our food.

When we were finished with the shelter for the night, which was a lark, we all scampered to the woods in search of fuel for both night and morning. We found an abundance of small sticks, but most of them were too water-soaked to give off much heat. It was the latter part of September, and the air was now quite chilly, especially at nighttime, so we built a huge bonfire of birch wood and a mixture of smaller branches. This open fire not only warmed our bodies, but the odor of burning wood and the very flames were food for our souls.

All this time, the men were working on the motor. We hoped that it would be functioning in the morning, but our faith in its ability to carry us upstream had been shattered by the afternoon's surprise stubbornness; we kept our fingers tightly crossed.

We slept in the one huge tent, but the entire space was covered when our individual rough beds were made, save a space in the corner for our camp stove. Each one of the group made his own bed. We were afforded the refreshing comfort of spruce boughs, which we gathered from the nearby trees. These branches served the purpose of springs. They were then covered with a reindeer skin, which was a substitute for a mattress and which also kept the dampness of the ground from our bodies.

What we had to eat that night has long been forgotten, except that we had pilot bread and tea, which were a delight to our ravenous guide. We hoped that he would bring down some game to help with our food supply, but the next morning he expended part of our ammunition with no results. This was alarming, for it was evident that at our present rate of travel, we couldn't possibly reach our destination in the five allotted days. Our guide didn't fully understand our language, but Mr. Kilbuck, who could converse in the Eskimo tongue, acted as an interpreter.

This was to be my first experience sleeping with a mixed crowd. We couldn't possibly carry more than one tent. It was a snug, cozy, folksy way, just one big happy family, but it didn't seem exactly the nice thing to do even though we slept in our clothes. The bed was hard, and the branches poking into my ribs took away some of the joy of traveling into this land of adventure. Even the babble of the river and the whistling wind didn't lull me to sleep. Finally, the climax to my uneasiness came when our guide, thinking we were all asleep, rose stealthily from his bunk, lifted the flap of the tent, and right there relieved himself.

The next morning we were rowing again, and trusting to luck to free us from our plight. It wasn't the least intriguing to row against the stream, making so little headway. We had no instruments for sending out an SOS, and we couldn't just sit on the riverbank and wait for help in that estrangement from the world.

God was with us even in the wilderness; our messages of mental telepathy must have been delivered, for we had no sooner started than we heard the dim droning of a motor in the near distance. It was coming our way, nearer and nearer, and then a boat rounded the bend so unexpectedly that we almost collided.

The owner was Mr. Johnson of the Northwest District, a master mechanic as well as an educator. He soon had our motor turning gently while we stood almost petrified in fear of its dying again, but in a very short time it was singing strongly "put-put-put." This sound was the sweetest music ever to our ears. We traveled that day without stress or difficulty. We kept going, rounding bend after bend, until the evening deepened into a dark, blue haze, for we did not dare turn off the motor lest the engine cool and refuse to act.

This speedier progress, with the motor behaving, quickly changed our spirits from gloom into sunshine and happiness. We enjoyed every turn in the river and were awake to the beauty of the universe, marveling at the grandeur of the Creator's handiwork so far in the North. Sometimes we sang; often we talked until we ran out of anything to say, and then we listened to the birds singing in the nearby, ever-changing woods.

Our second evening on the portage was spent at an old deserted fish camp. It seemed a dirty, smelly place to spend the night when we had passed so many inviting, clean spots along the way. Our leader defended his choice when he saw that we were all against his selection, and pointed out that here we would be supplied with fuel, water, and a frame for our tent. This was a great advantage and our objections were over-ruled—but it didn't help the smell. We always respected his judgment, however, for he was older and wiser in the ways of doing things in that country.

We went to work in earnest before the darkness prevented us from finding our equipment. The first night's practice helped us to finish our tasks quickly and more efficiently. We also sensed that our manager was somewhat impatient with us for being too slow in making and breaking camp.

We had been enjoying the life of lotus-eaters, but we knew that the circumstances required more speed, for an early winter would close navigation. We aimed to please and cooperate, since it was for our own good, so we worked faster and chattered less. There were no slackers or whiners in our party; the two fair maidens always put their shoulders to the wheel, regardless of how difficult the task might be.

That day we had purchased a salmon from a native family along the way, and now we scraped the scales, dressed it, and put it into a pot of salty water to boil. We had no recipe and no sauce, but it was delicious. Salmon caught in the cold, clear Alaskan waters can never be excelled.

We had hoped our native guide, who had a gun, would hit a duck, but he was a better guide than marksman, and we gave up hope of having any game on our journey.

From that day on we rationed our supplies.

About noon the next day we arrived at the first portage. Until this time the banks of the streams had hidden most of our view of the surrounding territory; now before our eyes were the boundless virgin prairies, called tundra, a strange and expansive country with a charm all its own; but it was somewhat lonely, for not a person lived in those parts.

There was nothing outstanding in the beauty of the portage, but the scene that left the most lasting impression on me was the awe-inspiring golden sunset across the tundra as the sun seemed to go down in a blaze of fire.

This portage was one of three to be hiked, and it was a mile long as the crow flies. A well-beaten path had been made through the timber most of the way, but in a few places the water would have percolated into my shoes had it not been for the fish-skin boots, clammy in appearance, that kept my feet dry. Occasionally a tree across our pathway required a detour in the mud.

We each carried our own baggage on the first trip and then returned for the reindeer skins and our blankets. One of the men transported the grub box, which was very much lighter than when we started on the journey; the other man was weighed down with the Evinrude. Finally, two extra trips were made to transport the boats. These were hoisted upside down, the men resting part of the heavy weight on their heads—and at last we were across the portage with all our paraphernalia.

We now fully understood why only bare necessities should be in our luggage, though right then a change of clothing would have added to my resolution. My foolish pride caused me to fret, yet it was useless worry, even though it was hard on my morale to be so messy, for we all looked more or less alike, and there was strength in numbers in the same predicament.

When the reindeer skins were wet, the hair came out in chunks; my reindeer skin was grayish in color, so my only suit, a navy blue serge, was soon covered with hair. My topcoat of like color was no longer recognizable. I even looked like a reindeer. It was evident that I would arrive at my teaching post in a dirty, dowdy, slovenly fashion.

Crossing the portage and taking time out to lunch had used the greater part of the day, so for the third night we made camp on the shore of a small lake, which we were to cross in the morning.

The next day was uneventful and we camped that night on the shore of a large body of water. It was a vast area, so that all we could see was water, wild and squally, with innumerable whitecaps. We were reminded of the sea, but here the tides didn't ebb and flow, and the force of the waves breaking on the shore was mild compared to the Pacific Ocean. This was the first night that we struggled with the odds against us in building a fire. It was difficult to find wood that wasn't soaking with water from a recent rain. We carried a starter of kindling in our pack, but this was used sparingly; even at that, the supply was fast being exhausted with each day's pittance.

Fortune frowned on us here for the second time; we spent two nights on the shore of this angry sea that defied our efforts to cross. The choppy water would have had no mercy on our small craft and any attempts to navigate would have ended in disaster; we had no choice but to wait for the storm to subside.

The third morning we awoke to a bright, blue sky free of water, for at last the redundant rain had ceased. The surface of the lake was still restless, but now there was no danger involved, though our light skiffs were easily tossed by the waves.

As we passed from the large lake into a smaller body of water, we were obliged to lay aside the tall reed grass with the oars to make a channel for the boats; consequently, this slowed our speed. This second lake was the source of a small stream, called Crooked Creek for its serpentine turns. In fact, it was so curved that the boat could scarcely make the bends without running into its banks. We followed this river dizzily for a short distance before we again ended the day's travel.

Recent travelers had spent the night here in a nearby depression similar to a wallow, for it was a windswept section with no shelter. This secluded hollow, protected from the wind, would be an ideal spot to rest, that is, if it didn't rain. A light shower would quickly turn such a basin into a puddle.

Rain was the furthest thing from our thoughts as we looked across the calm and serene lake that we had just crossed, and the sun went down in a blaze of crimson beyond the tundra. The sky was cloudless, the wind had come to a standstill, and the birds were singing their sweetest evening carols; we could imagine the music was staged in the nearby shrubs for our special pleasure—all was peace and joy.

But before morning we could hear the pitter-patter of rain on the roof of the tent—a restful sound, until the water began to fall in torrents; our little shelter was soon filled with muck and mire, and our bedding was soaked. It was "Hobson's choice" that we were off to an early start on a morning that was wet and cold with gray skies. The day was breaking in the east and there was light enough for us to load our canoes, for move we must—we didn't take time to brew our morning coffee.

My ten-dollar gold piece that I had saved out when I shopped in St. Michael had been wrapped securely, so I thought, and pinned to my shirt—a sort of bank for safekeeping. If my purse should be lost, I would at least not lose my money; but to my complete dismay, it had worn a hole, dropping into the tundra grass in the tent, and was hopelessly lost in the trampled mud and water. Our supply of kindling had also grown very low, we were almost out of food, and now my money was all gone.

Our spirits were tempered by the weather; yesterday we were on top of the world with sunshine and happiness in our souls; today we were in a slough of despondency without even a patch of blue in our skies. Cold feet and empty stomachs helped to lower the degree of our feelings, and the loss of my last cent remained at the back of my mind.

I was no little concerned over being exposed to so much dampness. I fully expected to be ill with pneumonia or to receive great distress from my chronic sinus; but to my great joy and peace of mind, the cold was gone, and the sinus with all its wheezes and sniffles, which had been a joy killer for years, was an ailment of the past—it has never returned to pester me again.

We three girls huddled under the tarpaulin to keep warm and dry, meanwhile nibbling on the last of the pilot bread to stay the pangs of hunger, while the men were exposed to the elements to keep the boat moving. The little motor seemed to be making up for lost time and compensating for the delay it had caused, as it impelled the boat around bend after bend with quickening speed down Johnson Creek. The rain and weather were becoming minor worries, for our food was all gone except a wee bit of rolled oats; our supply of tea was still plentiful, but that would afford little sustenance.

That night we camped on the last portage, one which was only a few hundred feet from stream to stream; here we moved over to the river called Mud Creek that was flowing in the direction of our destination. Fortune seemed to smile on us one day and frown on us the next. Life was a matter of ups and downs, and the things that caused the most worry never happened. That night we would have had no food, but before we had time to really suffer, a Captain Wallace Langley, who was going in the opposite direction on his way to the States for the winter, stopped at our camp overnight with food to spare.

The next night we were on the banks of the home stream, where we could feast our eyes on the beautiful Kuskokwim River. This river, with its magnetism and power, is a fast-moving body of water, for it is fed by the melting snow and ice of the Mount McKinley region together with the many, many sloughs that flow from all points of the compass to help swell its magnitude.

We camped on a high cliff overlooking the water, where a seventh person joined our ranks. This man most graciously offered to erect the tent and we happily consented, for we were getting somewhat tired of that sort of business—it had been a wonderful picnic, but by that time we had had our fill of the portage.

Our leader, Mr. Kilbuck, who now knew the country, sailed off into the sunset, much as did Hiawatha in his canoe, to buy potatoes and flour in a nearby village. When he returned with the ingredients, one of the girls made biscuits, making them on a camp stove for seven hungry people. The other lass boiled the potatoes and steeped the tea. Our meal lacked variety, but our hunger was satisfied and we were indeed thankful for food.

We were awakened in the middle of the night by a strong wind lashing our tent until it flapped and flapped; and then in the next split second it was whipped entirely off the poles—a sorry plight and most maddening. The man who had done the job of putting it up had a reputation in the country. He was known always to have a thousand dollars in his jeans and a valet to do his work, but this time the attendant was absent. It was quite evident that he had never put up a tent before, for it sagged in the middle and wasn't high enough to get around in with ease. We should have taken it down in the beginning, but we had respect for his feelings and appreciated his kindness in the attempt.

The next morning a launch lay at anchor to carry us on the homeward stretch with ease and comfort. Our manual labor had ended, for the captain had our baggage placed aboard the launch by a member of the crew. My possessions now consisted of a shedding reindeer skin, a steamer robe, a small overnight bag, and an empty purse.

Coffee was a most welcome change from the portage tea of the past few days; but we missed our supping Eskimo companion. He had turned back when we reached the divide in order to complete his homeward trip before it was too late for him to sail in his kayak. He had been a good scout, directing the way without fail.

We girls, who were a novelty in that area, were treated like queens, with every attention possible showered on us. Had I not been a member of a family with six brothers who never missed a chance to keep my ego cropped, all the consideration might have gone to my head. The other girls were already betrothed, and I was the only unattached white girl for miles and miles.

We were set to sail on this enchanting river, refreshed in body and spirit, when to our utter dismay, this engine refused to turn. They worked all that day, but the motor was evidently dead, and it wasn't until the next day that it began to churn and oppose the river. We reached Akiak in nine days instead of the scheduled five. The weather, engine trouble, and the fact that we girls were *cheechakos* (new in the country) caused the delay—Alaska sometimes teaches her people patience the hard way; nevertheless, it is a happy way to those who love the North.

Nearly six weeks of lagging travel from Seattle had ended. Today those same miles can be covered by aircraft in less than twenty-four hours. The view from the air is magnificent, for no other country can grant more awe-inspiring scenes, but the new thrills, the new friends, and the many new places of interest that we were privileged to know in our journey can never be enjoyed in just one day of travel. The ocean, the river, and even the portage with its peck of troubles I will always remember as an outstanding pleasure in my life.

CHAPTER 5

Arrival in Akiak

It was late when we landed in the white village in Akiak that evening; consequently, the first night was spent in one of the new homes with the girls. It was a relief to undress, to shed our corsets for the first time in several days, and to crawl into bed on a mattress with clean, white sheets and a soft, downy pillow. We felt that we had now returned to civilization with all its comfort—and a home-cooked meal.

This quiet little white village on the east side of the river afforded two stores of general merchandise and groceries, one of which was a combined roadhouse and store, and each was supplied with a roomy warehouse. Rows of cottages, built of either log or lumber, lined the riverbanks for a distance of a quarter of a mile, and other homes were built back among the trees. These houses were owned by the Laplanders in the reindeer industry and by the miners from various sections of that region. It was a ghost place in the summertime, when the families and the bachelors departed for the reindeer and mining camps.

The following day my few possessions and I were ferried to the west side of the river, though it was always east to me, for my directions were turned around. My home was to be in the native village for a year and perhaps longer—the word

"Akiak" means "across the river" in the native tongue. My one and only suit had been brushed and brushed until it now looked much better for the reception—I kept the skin among my souvenirs, though much of its hair was missing.

As I climbed the riverbank, the entire village was there to welcome their new teacher, "Lignoista," as they called me. Their salutations and greetings were in their Eskimo language, but they were sincere and kindly. They all stood in line to shake my hand.

Now anticipation became realization, and I found that conditions were to be quite different from the first plan. For instance, the new hospital, which was to have been completed by my arrival, was still little more than a dream; only the basement was finished. The lumber, doors, and windows were piled high around this hole in the ground, but later all this material was transferred to the church for safekeeping until spring. For some unknown reason, the lumber which was supposed to have been delivered on the first boat the previous spring didn't arrive until fall. It was then too late for work—the carpenter in charge had gone.

In place of my having a room in the new hospital and dining with the staff, I was to live in the bungalow which Mr. and Mrs. Kilbuck had formerly occupied. I was the only American "staff" in the village. Alice, the Kilbucks' maid, was to be my helper.

This government house was a most inviting home among the evergreen trees, with its low, sprawling gray-stained roof and wide overhanging eves. The wide, white sidingboards were placed up and down with narrow strips nailed over the seams to keep out the wind and cold. Three steps led up to a porch enclosed with a railing. On this enclosure were boxes of splashy yellow nasturtiums blooming profusely, even though it was the early part of October.

Alice, who was most cordial, was at the door with a smiling face to greet me, for she had been the caretaker during the summer. I couldn't speak her language, but she could well understand mine. At the same time, Prince and Shep, who were a part of the household, whined and woofed a time or two, then rose from their rag mats to welcome me with dignity, quite unlike the savage malamutes that would have taken a pound of flesh and enjoyed it if their chains had snapped as I came up the lane.

The home and school had at one time been under the same roof—a living room, bedroom, and tiny kitchen with a large ell attached to this section for a schoolroom. Then later a combined fruit and vegetable cellar was dug a few blocks away from this building, and over this basement was erected a cozy log schoolhouse. This huge ell schoolroom was then converted into a kitchen, and the tiny kitchen was used as a second bedroom.

One side of this oblong kitchen was entirely framed with windows, making the room light and airy and also letting in the view of the ever-interesting river and the massive mountains to the east. It was not only a kitchen, but also a utility room, and so immense that it was scrubbed each week for the cost of a dollar. The cupboards, cookstove, and dining table occupied one-half the space; a huge heater in the other end kept the entire room warm, and besides all this, Alice's bed and wardrobe were screened in one corner—this was her cozy nest where she sat at her work, humming a tune when she was in a singing mood.

The living room was pretty with its beamed ceilings and paneled walls of oak and cheerful cottage window. The furniture consisted of two oak morris chairs with leather cushions, a roll-back writing desk, and a bookcase made of seven rough milk boxes, three on one side and four on the other, nailed together and stained in oak. A wood heater stood near the wall between the two bedroom doors. A rag carpet on the floor reminded me of my early girlhood days on the farm.

The bedrooms were really one end of the living space partitioned with panels about seven feet high, so they were scene-proof but not soundproof. One of these rooms, which was much larger, was furnished with a double bed and a dresser. This was occupied by the nurse and me after she arrived. The other was smaller and colder, with a single bed and a chest of drawers, but it served a double purpose: it was Mr. Kilbuck's sleeping quarters when he came off the trail, and in the meantime it was used as a dispensary for the nurse.

The two collie dogs huddled around the kitchen stove on their rag mats with their bushy tails curled around their haunches—their skin didn't afford the same protection from the cold as did the fur of the native dogs. They had been sent into the country for the purpose of engendering other collies to be used in the reindeer camps, but for some reason the plan wasn't carried through and they were kept as pets. They were a most welcome part of the household.

Our home was built on a small knoll in the center of the shoestring village with a view of the massive mountains toward the east; native cabins or cottages extended several blocks to the north and the south. All the citizens owned their homes, which ranged in size from one to four rooms and which were built of logs from the nearby timber. The only underground structure was the council house, or *kashgee*. The little chapel was a frame building erected by the Moravian church. Our supplies were freighted across the river, since there was no store in our hamlet.

I had been in the village over a week, seeing no one but the native people, when a stranger came to our door—a woman dressed in a traveling outfit, with luggage. Who could she be? A surprised look must have registered on my face as she entered the door, for she immediately introduced herself, saying, "I am Mrs. Evans, the government nurse."[6] Then she continued, "Sorry, I am not the young, beautiful redheaded nurse whom you met in Seattle." Quickly I answered, "I am very happy to welcome you." As she removed her hat and coat she continued, "The doctor and nurse canceled their contract when they heard the hospital wasn't ready for operation."

Mrs. Evans was tired and hungry, having just arrived over the Yukon portage. Her cheeks looked hollow and she had deep circles under her eyes. I immediately offered her hot coffee to revive her. Dinner was ready and Alice set an extra plate. Alice had been dining with me, as was her custom with Mr. and Mrs. Kilbuck. The nurse seemed to frown her disapproval at this, but I thought, "Change it if you can. You don't know Alice."

Mrs. Evans, who was in her late thirties, had a girlish figure. She was quick of action, neat as a pin, and walked in a proud, dignified manner. Her eyes were big and blue; her auburn hair, which she brushed a hundred strokes each day, was smoothly rolled in a knot on the top of her head. She was kind and considerate, but she could sometimes speak sharply. I was from Kansas, she from California, but she too had been born in Kansas, and had been taken to the West Coast as a tiny infant.

Mr. Kilbuck had remained in the village long enough to officiate at the weddings of both Betty and Ruby; then he hurried to Goodnews Bay before the ice came. Mrs. Evans soon left to inspect the health of a lower village.

Alice was a good-looking Eskimo with a large, flat face that bore lines of character and with white teeth that enhanced her beauty when she smiled. A shampoo at least once a week kept her coarse, lustrous black hair immaculate, and never a lock was out of place; she was meticulous in her dress and sewed her clothing with her own hands in modern fashion. Her face radiated happiness most of the time, but she was not consistently cooperative.

Mrs. Kilbuck, who was a capable, home-loving person, had trained Alice to do everything in the line of housework, and she did her teacher justice in doing everything well. She could cook, wash, iron, and keep the house in perfect order, when she was in the right spirit, and was the only one of the like in that community; on the other hand, she could be the very devil incarnate if the impulse of the moment inspired her to it.

When possessed with one of her periodical tantrums she would blurt out, "Me no speak English. Me no savvy white folks," and with that out of her system she would stalk furiously to "me papa's house," which was her father's home—he was the chief of the village.[7] Sometimes she merely hid away without giving a reason. When this particular fit of temper cooled she would return, bubbling over with joy and seemingly more industrious than before. She was always glad to return, but it wasn't through repentance, though once in a long while she would say, "Me solly."

She was much in demand as a baker, for she could deliver the best bread without an equal—and the worst. On one occasion the territorial marshal asked her to have ten loaves of bread baked for him at the end of the week. He was going on a prospecting trip. She must have harbored a grudge against this man, for when the bread was delivered and the cost paid, he opened the carton, hurling the loaves, which were harder than rocks, to the dogs. Then with a sardonic grin she said, "Me plenty mad at white man. Me leave out the yeasta."

Alice had been twice married at this date; she had first been joined in matrimony by a common-law marriage, which her parents had prearranged, to an Aleut on the Aleutian Islands at the tender age of twelve. This wedded life was of short duration, for her husband very soon died of a plague that cut down most of the village. Sometime later she was found in a lonely, dark igloo near death mostly from starvation. Her physique and determination probably saved her life, for her physical stamina was almost unbelievable—but if only the good die young, she wouldn't be on the eligible list. She was twice relegated to the status of widowhood without children, for her second husband was a victim of tuberculosis, a disease that has long been prevalent among the natives in Alaska.

The opening of school was delayed for two weeks, for the children had not yet returned from their summer stay at the fish camps. This was fortunate, since it gave me a chance to attend the wedding festivities and also time to unpack the generous supply of provisions the government had sent for both home and school.

In our supplies was a gift from the gods—a bolt of blue and white percale to be used in the school sewing—what a find! Neither the nurse nor I had any change of dress since neither of our trunks would follow until spring. We immediately took possession of most of this material with no compunctions of conscience. The material was ample, with some left over, for three complete outfits for each of us. They were all made from the same pattern in uniform style with white cuffs and collars.

My worries about being penniless were over. Now we had clothing, and the trader sold our groceries on a monthly basis; the lights, house, and fuel were supplied by the government, so all my material wants were gratified.

Teaching school and managing a home kept me well occupied. The school couldn't be neglected, for that was my first duty, but the house was sometimes disordered. I had been my mother's helper, but assisting was quite a different matter from being entirely responsible, so there was much to learn.

Saturday was the day set aside to do the baking, and in addition, we cleaned and dusted the house, which was a big order. If everything wasn't done exactly as Mrs. Kilbuck had done it, Alice was angered and quickly raised her voice in opposition, saying, "Mrs. Kilby, no—Mrs. Kilby, no, no."

The dirt from the mukluks soon soiled the carpet here and there and especially where people stood to hug the stove. To remove the tacks and lift the furniture was a man-size job. One day, to avoid so much extra work, I asked Alice to have the room well heated and then scrub the rag carpet with Fels Naptha and hot water as it lay on the floor. At this she fairly screeched, "Mrs. Kilby, no!" I became as angered as she. I started the task myself, while she sat in a comfortable rocking chair, sneering at my efforts. When she saw that my way was really bringing results, she then, much to my surprise, finished the cleaning herself, with some respect for my way of doing things.

We tried to keep the place clean and tidy, for we never knew when to expect people from over the trail, especially since there were no telephones to give us a minute's warning—our teakettle was always on the stove to serve chilled travelers a piping hot drink.

My first invited guest caused me to be a bit jittery, for nothing seemed to be in order that Friday evening, and I was tired from a trying day in the schoolroom. I didn't know that Alice had gone on one of her periodical pouting sprees until the piecrust was ready to roll. Then I found the rolling pin and other articles missing, including her Haviland china cup and saucer, the eggbeater, and the measuring cup. These were her special possessions, which didn't belong to the government supplies. These few utensils went with her when she was feeling contrary, but likewise came back when she was again in a happy frame of mind.

A vinegar bottle would serve the purpose of a rolling pin, and she must never know that she and her possessions were ever missed or that my plans were ever thwarted by her chicanery.

My temperature must have gone up from this unexpected vexation, for when the biscuits were ready for the oven, I remembered—no baking powder. This batch of dough was quickly hidden out of sight on the top shelf of the cupboard, and another lot speedily mixed.

It wouldn't ordinarily have been a cause for concern, but my guest was the head of our division, from St. Michael, and my reputation as a new teacher was at stake.

Roast duck was going to be the entree for the dinner, a gift from a hunter passing our way. I had prepared the ducks

Akiak, as seen from the air, about 1930. The Eskimo village is on the far side of the river. (Courtesy of James H. Barker.)

The teacher's house and garden at Akiak.
(Photograph by the Reverend Ferdinand Drebert.
From the collection of Dorothy Zimmerman.)

John Kilbuck and students at the Akiak school, 1915. These children would have been May's students the following year. (Courtesy of the Yugtarvik Regional Museum, Bethel, Alaska.)

beforehand, stuffed them with dressing, and put them in the oven, so that worry was over with—so I thought. I had hoped that everything would go off like a charm—but it didn't. The ducks had lived on fish, and when I opened the oven door the aroma was overpowering to say the least—the taste was most sickening.

I was told later that the embarrassing situation could have been saved if the ducks had soaked in saltwater or stuffed with dried apples overnight, but it was one of those perplexing moments of the inexperienced—even the oven reeked of fish for days.

Most of the days were happy ones with everything operating smoothly, but sometimes, as in the week of the fishy duck, everything seemed to work against me. It was comforting to have the nurse return after a fortnight of absence from the village, for she was a sustaining influence. The superintendent,

The nurse, Lulu Evans Heron (left), about 1918.
Mrs. Heron served as a nurse in the Bethel region into the 1940s.
Also in the picture are Mrs. John Felder and her daughter,
Margaret. John Felder was a partner in the store at Akiak.
(Photograph by John Felder. Courtesy of the Yugtarvik
Regional Museum, Bethel, Alaska.)

Chief Kawagaleg and his wife. He was also the Moravian helper at the Akiak church. (Photograph by the Reverend Ferdinand Drebert. Courtesy of the Moravian Archives, Bethlehem, Pa.)

Mr. Kilbuck, who was a morale builder, too, came back from a long trip a few days later. Finally, Alice slipped in the back way, rather sheepishly for having deserted the place the last few days, so now our family was complete.

There was little time for play or an afternoon siesta in my routine, for every day was brimful and running over with work. As a result, I slept the sleep of the righteous.

Playing the church organ and checking out the reindeer supplies were tacked onto my duties, so there was really no time for homesickness or loneliness. The sermon was delivered in the native tongue, and the hymns had been translated into the Eskimo language, but the music was familiar—being the same tunes that we sang in our little home church. The services were usually long and boring, especially when the village chief presided, for he kept on talking until his lengthy dissertation was ended.

Since the sermon was not understandable, it occurred to me that this would be an opportune time to write my letter home and save time wasted in nervous energy; seeing this action, the minister chided me for being so irreverent in the place of worship. Jokingly I told him that I was merely taking notes on his sermon, but he so resented this self-centered act that I finally wrote my letters at home.

It was definitely a pleasure to deal out the supplies to the jovial, red-faced reindeer herders, but often there was no interpreter available, so I had to learn the Eskimo name for each article in the store in order to understand their wants and serve them more efficiently. All reports were mailed to the government.

CHAPTER 6

The School

The children enjoyed attending school, for there was little of interest in that country to divert their attention, or to encourage them to play hooky. If the pupils were ill or absent for a legitimate reason, the mothers sent a written excuse, formulated by someone who could read and write the English language. When a seat was vacant we knew that for some reason incidents out of the ordinary had taken place.

Shortly after the beginning of the fall term, we saw black smoke gushing from the schoolhouse chimney flue. Usually the older boys assumed the responsibility of looking after the heater, but this was Saturday. Evidently something out of the usual procedure must have happened or the schoolhouse was on fire. In every corner of both home and school hung a pyrene extinguisher to be used in time of need; I grabbed one of these mechanical devices and rushed outside, half-dressed, to meet the emergency. I felt that my life was about to ebb out with heart failure, caused by all this unusual excitement. I felt a great responsibility in the care of the government property, since a burned building in that country wasn't easily replaced.

When I arrived at the scene, the children sat in their individual seats, looking shy yet impish. Then with one accord they hastened to say, "Lignoista, we want school; we want school today. Please."

Who ever heard of children attending school on a Saturday merely for pleasure? Usually, it was quite the reverse. I was angry because they were the instigators of all this unwanted alarm, but on the other hand, it was most satisfying to have them so assiduous as to yearn for school even on a holiday. My temper was under control, and they were not even scolded. We compromised by singing a few songs, which was their delight, and the session was dismissed for the day.

One overgrown boy, named Ivan, came from a tundra village to enter school for the first time. Seeing that his ears were partly frozen, I asked him where he had slept and if he had eaten his breakfast. He answered, to my surprise, in broken English, "Me sleep in kashga. Me not eat." He was sent to our table for breakfast, and Alice was quite proud of him because he gave thanks for the food before he had eaten—little did he have to be thankful for in his way of life. It was bordering on forty below, and all he had to wear, besides his parka, were shabby pants and a shirt with a slit down the back. He was an orphan with no real home, so I bought him a pair of blue denim pants and a woolen suit of white underwear. In addition, I gave him one of my good, blue woolen sweaters that was too small for me.

The next morning when I entered the schoolroom, he was sitting in his seat bedecked in his white underwear, grinning from ear to ear with happiness, and gratitude was written all over his face. It was a laughable, yet pathetic, sight. I asked him what had happened to the rest of his clothes and he hastened to reply, "Me papa like me pants. Me mama like me sweater." They were his aunt and uncle who lived in the village. Since this was true, I said, "You go at once for your clothes." He did, and came back dressed.

The school was especially interesting, but it was, indeed, a distinct contrast from past experiences. The children learned the three Rs and the things that would be useful to them in everyday living; they were taught with emphasis the value of money. The boys enjoyed manual training, while the girls learned to sew, knit, and cook. The government furnished the supplies for the domestic arts.

They were always happy when Friday came, because they could sketch and watercolor. Singing was a pleasure, for they had music in their souls.

The nurse came quite often to inspect their health and to teach them cleanliness and the care of their bodies.

These pupils were a quiet, somber, dreamy group, and I often wondered what was uppermost in their thoughts. Their faces were noticeably flat, but rosy cheeked and chubby; they had dark skin, dark eyes, and dark, straight, coarse hair, except for a freak of nature. The frame of their body was small, with dainty hands and feet.

The children insisted on sitting in the schoolroom wearing their parkas, and it was like pulling teeth to get them to remove these furs—they were just a part of them, and they felt undressed without them.

They were never demonstrative; kissing was definitely not an indulgence and nose rubbing was a rare occurrence—perhaps a good trait for the sake of health. One of the miners tried to tease a schoolboy by saying, "Jimmy, Miss Wynne said that you kissed Katie at school one day." He was furious and shouted, "Lignoista, she lie for me."

Out in front of our huge, bright window was the rendezvous for the children each evening. Here they met with their ivory story-knives to depict exciting stories in the snow: the tale might be of a man in a fight with a bear to save his life, and the various means that he planned to escape. It could be of a quarrel between a man and his wife, and the thwarted developments in the reconciliation, or just anything in the community life or the history of the race, but they would spend happy hours in this way of amusement.

Discipline was no problem whatsoever, for they hadn't learned all the mischief of the modern youth, but were truly thankful to advance without heckling the teacher.

Their not knowing the English language was a handicap. Sometimes all my care and eagerness seemed to accomplish little, for at times they crept up the scale of learning with painful slowness; but eventually, like the tortoise, they made the goal in the end, even though a few of the number were two years in the grade.

The girls were great imitators, and it was only a short time until my likeness could be seen in their hair and dress. They soon wore short sleeves, but left their underwear showing below the elbow; even the chief's wife, a very wrinkled old lady, cut her sleeves short, and she, too, left her underwear dangling, which didn't improve her appearance in the least.

Most of the children came to school neatly clothed with clean bodies, but there were a few of the unfortunate infected with lice in their hair and clothing. If a pupil spied a louse wandering aimlessly on the hair or neck of the person in the seat ahead, he would reach up, capture it, crush it between his thumbnails, and proceed unconcerned with his work—a daily occurrence. We made the effort to rid them of these parasitic insects, but in most cases our attempts were futile, for it was necessary to go to the very source of the dilemma—their home life. The government had sent a large supply of chloronaphthalene, a liquid which my father used as a sheep dip, to be used in killing lice. This killed the nits and brought them out of their hiding places. The children wanted to be rid of these cooties to be eligible for the honor list, but they submitted themselves to the ordeal of a shampoo reluctantly, for they despised the sting and odor of this cootie killer. One mother rather resented our efforts, for she believed that lice were essential to good health.

One of the pupils was celebrating a birthday. We gave a surprise tea party for him at the noon hour in the schoolroom.

A white lady, Mrs. Omen,[8] sent sandwiches made of bread with caraway seeds. The bread was delicious, fresh out of the oven, but none of the children would touch them. What was wrong? Finally, one little girl dared to speak, "We no likum. We no eat bread with lice!"

There were several orphan children in the village, who were sadly neglected. In the fall we placed a box in each of the stores across the river for the purpose of collecting castaway clothing. We had no special name for our philanthropic idea like the Salvation Army, or the St. Vincent de Paul, but we did save some of the children from being cold by making over discarded wearing apparel.

A sewing club was formed to meet one night each week to sew for these neglected children. Fathers and mothers would care for their own offspring, but those bereft of parents often suffered. They felt the lack of love and care especially at Christmastime when others were bedecked for the festivities. That fall our club made six complete outfits, and gave six tub baths; but the joy was never greater than when we looked at the happy faces of the children, who were victims of circumstances through no fault of their own.

One of our community projects was to rid the village of all the tin cans that had been opened and then dumped into a pile or even scattered here and there. These were transported to the river in a wheelbarrow or sled, along with any other useless, discarded rubbish, to go out with the ice in the spring.

The time included in this cleanup often covered part of several days, but the effort changed our village from a dump pile to a place of beauty when nature arrived in the spring with her handiwork.

CHAPTER 7

Friends

It wasn't until I had reached my station that I fully understood what Mother Superior had been trying to impress upon me. She didn't predict that I would lower my standards of conduct, for she knew I had a firm set of values. If a woman looks for dishonor it is forthcoming; if she expects to be treated with respect and esteem, in no country will her wishes be so richly granted.

The men I met were all somewhat older than I, but they were not predatory, as Mother Superior had warned. They were genuine bighearted, chivalrous characters with no visible signs of selfishness, shallowness, or hell-bound ways. In like manner, they were broad-minded, with a largeness of heart that I had never met before.

They left nothing undone to make my stay pleasant. The food cache was always filled with surprises; it might be a hind quarter of reindeer or a chunk of bear meat; sometimes it was a rabbit or a bag of geese, but my larder never lacked for meat.

My bachelor friends were all different and all likable. Joe Venus made me a picture sled; George Olson and Karl Smith brought over any special goodies that might come into the store.[9] Jack Heron, the United States commissioner, a noble, praiseworthy character who was a Canadian by birth, was my handyman. When the stovepipes were filled with soot, he emptied the contents; when it was time for the storm windows, he saw that they were in place; whenever the door refused to close, he planed the edges until they swung back as usual. Besides all this, he was the carpenter when the schoolroom required ventilators. His dignity seemed above these kindnesses, but he didn't seem to mind doing them, and he was a prize friend.

One of my most delightful experiences was learning how to handle skis. A friendly man, whose name I have forgotten, from his own ingenuity fashioned, seasoned, and waxed two pairs of skis that afforded me much pleasure on the nearby hills. There was no ski lift to relieve the long, tedious climb to the top, but the run down was all the better.

Another outstanding friend was an Englishman, Percy Goodair, a man of medium height with graying hair cut in a pompadour fashion. When he was down from the hills, he often came to call and sometimes stayed for dinner. We went for walks in the fresh air up the trails bordered by the evergreen trees. He came with all the dignity of an English lord, for he had a title. There was something very impressive about this princely man. We were always accompanied on these walks by our mutual friend, Ole, who acted as chaperone, and his two beautiful dogs were his constant companions, even on our hikes. No one knew why a man of his caliber was prospecting in the hills and living in a tent, but I knew him as an interesting character and excellent company. In the spring he returned to England to serve his country in the war.

Only once did any of the men receive a "right down" dirty reception when they came to call, and that was soon after my arrival in the village. These three men, Bishop, Omen, and Heron, were tops in the country. All three stood over six feet in stature and had a common interest in the alluring game of mining.

Just as they entered the living room one evening, something

must have snapped, for down came all the stovepipes, filled with soot, crashing to the floor in a horrible mess. These pipes led through the bedroom, fifteen feet or more, to join the kitchen heater. The Saturday cleaning had just been finished and the kitchen scrubbed. Now even the shiny medicine bottles were covered with black soot—worse than they had been in the Mount Katmai eruption of 1912, which did send some of its cinders that distance.

It was fortunate for us that they came at this time, for it took these strong men only a very short while to clean up the soot and replace the pipes with new wiring. To show our deep appreciation for their kindness in setting the house in order once again, we invited them to stay for dinner; the disheartening episode was then soon forgotten—save for a layer of soot, high and low, for days.

The ladies as well as the men were wonderful people to know, and I was greatly impressed with their character and high standards of behavior. Often was I reminded of our last visit to the steamer *Victoria* as she was returning to Seattle. We had gone to the ship to bid the returning fellow passengers good-bye, when one tourist, a round-tripper, said to me as we were going down the gangway, "I can imagine that you will be happy to return to the States where you can associate with decent women." That was a stupid remark to be made at any time, and so often I was reminded of his ignorance. Never in my life have I been privileged to associate with a finer type of people or people with higher ideals.

It's true that there were a few loose-living girls, whose morals had long since died, who followed the camps to make money, and to satisfy the natural functions of men. These women of ill fame lived in a world of their own and apart from other people, in the cabins called the "row." Perhaps their ratio in this so-called "red-light" district was no greater than in the world at large.

CHAPTER 8

A Death and a Funeral

The doors of our house were never locked, for a very good reason. We couldn't find the keys, though we searched in every conceivable place. We sifted all the drawers that held a little bit of everything from mousetraps to keys, but the right key to the door was missing. Sometimes in the wee small hours of the night when strange noises were heard that gave one the shivers—illusive sounds on the doorstep, the lonely, whistling wind, spruce trees slapping against the windows—or when I had to stay alone, a locked door would have provided a secure, protected feeling.

White people always knocked and then waited to be admitted before entering, but the natives often barged into the house unannounced. They considered rapping an unnecessary exertion and a waste of time, an especially silly custom in the severe cold weather.

One night very late in midwinter, a native mother stood at the foot of my bed calling, "Lignoista, Lignoista, my little boy, Willie, plenty sick—you come quick." With these foreboding words she turned, left the room, and hurried away. In the quiet of the night her footsteps could be heard on the crunching snow as she scurried back to her home and the sick child.

She must have awakened me from a deep sleep. I hopped

out of bed, bewildered and half-dazed, dressing in double-quick time. The room was warm with the firelight still flickering and flashing through the isinglass door, but shadows were lurking in the corners.

What could I do? There was no telling what was the matter with him. I grabbed the first-aid kit and followed in her wake, wishing that I knew something about medicine besides giving a dose of castor oil. The nurse was out of the village, so it was my duty to go, even if only for moral support. Prince and Shep were more awake than I, with their noses in the door to go with me. Somehow they sensed the seriousness of the call. They never let me go alone in the daytime and now it was after midnight. Walking with two collies as my aides, I felt secure although no lamps were lighted in any of the houses, and it seemed awfully dark with just a flashlight to guide the way.

At that time of year a few trusty dogs were not chained. As we dashed through the village, scarcely awake, four of these loose animals came bounding after us, barking in a terrible, vicious manner; all the dogs on chains echoed their refrain in the peace of the night. Had I not been thoughtless in running, perhaps they wouldn't have noticed my presence. Prince and Shep did their utmost to protect me, thrusting their sharp teeth in the huskies' legs and jumping on their necks, while I grabbed a stick near the path to defend myself as best I could. We were outnumbered three to four and I feared for my life. Luckily, a villager heard my screams and the yelping dogs and came hurriedly to the rescue. It was a narrow escape.

Most of the people in the village had faith in the government worker, and in the modern medicine that he administered; otherwise they wouldn't have disturbed my peaceful slumbers in the small hours of the night. A few old-timers still believed that the medicine man had been given supernatural powers in healing and that he could heal them or see what was in store for them in the future or explain the cause of all their past. The younger generation had risen above these superstitions, so this mother naturally came for my help.

When I reached the home, breathless—and scared to death because I felt so helpless in a need so grave—it was too late to be of any assistance. A little boy of seven years, pale and deathly quiet, lay in a homemade bunk in one corner of the large room. The family sat with bowed heads, and a look of despair and sorrow registered on all their faces, for the child was just breathing his last.

It was my first experience of seeing someone die. I cried and my heart ached, for life had just begun for him. In those early days adolescents had little chance of living a long life; too many were doomed to an early death, principally through three factors. Parents often intermarried, cousins married cousins, and whole villages were related through marriage in one way or another. Then, too, their food lacked the necessary vitamins for good health, and often the quantity wasn't sufficient for them to grow and ward off disease at the same time. And many of the homes were one-room cabins, so naturally they lived in very close confinement and usually a member of the family was ill with tuberculosis. For these reasons the youth faded quickly, and only the rugged survived the pitfalls of childhood.

The body was taken by friends to the little chapel, which had been the scene of many funerals, to lie in waiting until all preparations were made for the final burial. Sometimes the remains were left alone in the church overnight, which to me was cold-blooded. In my girlhood days it was the custom for two or three friends to keep wake all night, or until the funeral was over. The departed was beyond all earthly harm, but it was a kind token of respect not to leave him alone so soon in death.

The next day a spirit of sadness and gloom prevailed throughout the community and signs of grief were displayed in different ways. Some of the older ladies pulled their hair down over their faces and left it uncombed for some time. This was an old custom of showing their grief and sorrow.

The villagers went ahead with the grim business of a funeral; it was wintertime and the earth was frozen hard as a rock, making grave digging a very difficult task. The ground had to be chiseled and thawed, with two or three men working steadily the entire day before the opening was the required depth. This was a trying job in the severe cold, and consequently, the men worked in relays.

Other men made the coffin of lumber that was kept in reserve in the attic of the church especially for caskets. They were most artistic in covering the coffin with fabric supplied by the trader across the way, which he had in stock for emergencies, such as this unexpected death—we marveled at the beauty of their work, but "necessity is the mother of invention."

After the funeral service was ended in the church, the pallbearers carried the coffin outside, where the family gathered around the tilted, open casket for a picture of the departed with them in the background. This was a convention seldom missed, even on a dark day, when there was scarcely light enough for a portrait.

These native people live a much simpler, quieter life than our way of living, but they have the same hopes and sorrows; and the loss of this little boy was deeply mourned. They didn't grieve as long as we do when our loved ones are taken; neither were they as extreme in laughter or sorrow. They take what life has in store for them without bemoaning their fate; indeed, they are sad, but do not carry on by loud crying and wailing.

When the last sad rites were ended, and the departed lowered into the grave, all the few earthly possessions were then placed on top of the casket. Among the articles were his bedding, clothing, and cooking utensils, with sufficient food to last him until he reached the happy hunting ground.

Before the grave was covered, the mourners had turned and gone on their way about the business of living, seeming from all outward appearance to have forgotten their loss and sorrow. This evidently is the stoic way of life for the Eskimo as well as the Indian, but it takes strength of character to go forward and not look backward without heartaches.

CHAPTER 9

The Moravian Chapel

Most of the social life of the community centered around the little Moravian church, a denomination that had been directing the religious activities in the Kuskokwim region since 1885 with headquarters in Bethel, Alaska. Churchgoing in this village was especially heavy, and it was unusual for a person to be absent from any service if he were at all able to attend. When the chapel bell rang, the villagers dashed out of their homes, swiftly hurrying to the church. I was reminded of the pictures of our Pilgrim families; yet, the Eskimo dress was most different in style, and it wasn't necessary to shoulder a gun to protect themselves from the Indians while they were worshiping.

Thanksgiving, Christmas, and Easter were major events in the life of the church, both religiously and socially. In the fall when the rabbits were plentiful, the natives and whites together joined in a rabbit hunt two days before Thanksgiving for meat to be served at this harvest festival; however, when the rabbits grew scarce, a reindeer from one of the herds was barbecued.

Roasting this animal whole was a delicious way of cooking the meat, and moreover, it warranted an ample supply for the large number that assembled for this event. Early in the fall, at least before the ground had frozen for the winter, a deep pit had been excavated to a depth of nearly six feet for this special occasion. When the logs that had been placed in this lacuna had burned to deep, glowing coals, the dressed carcass was hoisted on a frame over the pit; it usually required about eight hours of cooking before the meat was tender. Naturally, the man who was responsible for this part of the feast was up at an early hour in order to be ready to serve when the church services ended at midday.

All the people on both sides of the river had a share in the preparation of this potluck feast, and here again they could be likened to the Pilgrims. The few white women in the community did themselves proud, for the table was laden with good things to eat—roast reindeer, gravy, assorted jellies, pickles and vegetables from their own gardens, Alice's super home-made bread fresh out of the oven, scalloped oysters, ice cream, all kinds of pies and cakes—and one lady never thought a festive dinner was complete without a dish of lima beans. No banquet in the States could have been more plentiful or more delicious.

The natives furnished their own ice cream, which was made in a different manner from ours, or at least with other ingredients, namely, snow, berries, and seal oil, mixed, then left to freeze. Some of the whites pretended to like this dish, but one whiff of the seal oil, which released an odor resembling bad eggs, was sufficient for most of them.

Long tables were placed in the center of the church, where the white people were seated; then, in contrast, the Eskimos lined the walls, sitting on the floor, with the church pews serving as tables. This was their favorite way of relaxing and dining in their homes. Even Eskimo women who marry white men sit on the floor to eat their food, while their husbands dine at a table.

When everyone present was served to his fill, the remaining

food was then given to the poor and needy of the village; and those who were too ill to attend in person were most generously remembered in their homes.

The next big festivity was Christmas, and it was truly the highlight of the year, since all the reindeer men, who had spent most of the time in the camps, would then return to the village to enjoy the holiday with their families. While here, they not only gave pleasure to their own immediate homes, but they also created a spirit of laughter and a lively good time in the community, for they were endowed with more life and activity than the men who lolled around the village year in and year out.

It was a land of Christmas trees, so it wasn't at all difficult to select from the open tundra two well-proportioned evergreens for the church. They were erected, one on each side of the pulpit, and then the young people decorated them beautifully with trimmings which had been saved from year to year. Candles were placed on the tree to add to the Christmas spirit, but for the sake of safety they were never lighted.

A program was presented in the chapel, sponsored jointly by the church and school, in which everyone worked faithfully to make it a success; and eventually all breathed a sigh of relief, when it was over, that is, if it were rendered smoothly with no one forgetting his lines.

No gifts were placed on the tree for anyone, thus avoiding the unhappiness of someone being slighted in the inequality of giving presents; but on the other hand, each child was generously remembered with fruits, candies, and nuts, which made their eyes sparkle and gave a pain in the stomach to those who gobbled it all down at once.

Holy Week was always set aside for religious services in the church, which everyone reverently attended, but it was a decided contrast from the gaiety of Thanksgiving and Christmas, for at this time there was much fasting and little feasting. Then when Lent was over and the Easter services had ended on Sunday, the natives could be seen, going and coming, here and there, carrying a particular gift or some special dish of food to a dear friend; and they were usually mindful of those who were ill. These motives were permeated with the spirit of friendship and goodwill.

CHAPTER 10

I Adopt an Eskimo Orphan

Late one evening, unexpectedly and much ahead of schedule, Mr. Kilbuck arrived over the trail with his sled and reindeer, his customary way of traveling in the wintertime. This slow, snaillike means of transportation, provided by the government, was an inexpensive way for him to drive from place to place, to schools, reindeer camps, or wherever his many duties might call him. Obviously, there was nothing expeditious in this method of conveyance; as a result he was sometimes long overdue, and again he might arrive beforehand, but sooner or later he reached his destination—living by the clock or even the calendar was definitely out of the picture in Alaska.

There could be many reasons for delay, including stormy weather, a lame deer, or unfinished business, but the most vital of all was the time taken out to feed the deer. While the driver slept, the animal was pastured on the tundra, where he dug beneath the snow for moss, his food—the snow being his drinking water.

We watched Mr. Kilbuck as he walked proudly, following his sled up the lane to the village. He resembled Santa Claus, in that snow-laden region, for he was dressed in furry clothes, with an ice-covered beard; however, he lacked the little round belly, for he was straight of stature and tall.

When he stopped his reindeer, the villagers gathered around him in great commotion with smiles and much hand-shaking, for they were sincerely glad to see him and, more especially, since this hamlet had been his home for years; then, too, he carried greetings from relatives and friends from the places where he had been; and in addition to all these people there was a herder who immediately took charge of his deer for the night. Finally, when all present were given a chance to extend greetings and ask their questions, he started for the house.

It was then that our curiosity was greatly aroused, for he carried not only his luggage, but to our surprise, a tiny child snuggled close in his one arm. This child, less than three years old, was an orphan whom he had found living with relatives in a downriver village near Goodnews Bay. Strangely enough, in this home she was unwanted, neglected, and most urgently in need of another home. Besides not being welcome, she had suffered inhuman treatment at the hands of a mean, ignorant, and merciless aunt. It was scarcely believable but she had been placed purposely on a hot stove for punishment, a torturous treatment that had left a brand on her hips which she would carry all her life.

Since both of her parents had died, she was obliged to make her home with relatives. Orphan children among many of the older Eskimos are treated as outcasts and made the servants for the family of which they are a part—this wicked aunt was exceptionally heartless.

This was the psychological moment for the superintendent to ask a favor, while our sympathies for the child were soaring; he was a man of very few words and lost no time in saying, "Could you take care of her for a few days?" In the same breath he added, "I am sure that Alice will be willing to tend her while school is in session."

Playing the role of a mother to a baby would be a new experience, but my day was already brimful and running over with all the duties tacked onto school teaching; however, since the favor was asked for only a few days, it must be tackled with enthusiasm; and besides, if there was any human kindness in my blood there was no other way out but to graciously acquiesce.

The days came and the days passed and still she remained with us, for finding a home for a child required an extensive search. We all conjectured as to what efforts he had put forth to have her cradled elsewhere, but it was the general conclusion that he hadn't made much of an attempt. She was in good care. We were supposed to be imbued with the benign and benevolent spirit in every way.

She was called Lily. Just why she was christened with that name was most perplexing, since she resembled a lily in no way whatsoever. Her little baby head was covered with straight, black, coarse hairs, all in tangles and dirty from lack of care; her face was scared, sad, and flat, with a little pug nose; furthermore, her swarthy body was thin and frail from want of nourishing food. While she was shy and bashful, she seldom cried, but her somber face presented a dark picture of sadness. The benevolence in our souls was awakened to her in love and sympathy. She had a right to live and that with love and comfort.

She continued to be my baby, winning her way deeper and deeper into the affections of my heart each day, and her appearance soon changed; food took away the emaciated look, and soap and water and clean, fresh clothes worked wonders for her appearance; then in time she overcame her fear, developing into a distinctive character with sweet, childish ways.

She gave us little trouble for a child of her years. Alice, however, often complained because she wet her bed; this was, indeed, a problem for immediate and speedy solution, for Alice did the laundry each week. It was icy cold weather and drying wet bedding in the kitchen did not fill the atmosphere with a very agreeable aroma. Whatever the cost, peace and harmonious relations were necessary, for if Alice went on strike we would be in a serious predicament.

Something had to be done about the situation, but I was inexperienced in the methods of child care, and didn't have the heart to execute a spanking, for her little body had already suffered enough welts. If she were well and if love and care with reason didn't bring results, then there would be no other course to follow but to let her sleep in her wet, uncomfortable bed, while nature took its course. Often she tried our patience in the training, but after much work and worry, she ultimately graduated from that stage of life.

Sewing had always been one of my favorite hobbies; for that reason it was a pleasure to plan, fashion, and make her clothes. I also knit her socks and sweaters, and since she was so tiny a garment could be finished in a short time. Alice, too, enjoyed making her fur clothing from some of the skins furnished by the government for special needs.

CHAPTER 11

The Reindeer Fair

The Reindeer Fair for western Alaska was a novel event that took place shortly after the first of the year, and our village of Akiak was the scene of lively activity.[10] The deer selected for the occasion were brought down from the pasture lands over the frozen winter trails. Each herder attempted to rival the other men in presenting the best-groomed reindeer, the finest woven sled, and super-made harness, while he himself was attired in new fur clothing especially planned for this gala annual celebration.

Sourdoughs, even a few white women, came from far and near to be present for the exhibition. The roadhouse across the river was filled to capacity, but our house always seemed to have room for just one more.

School was closed for one entire week, but even so, it wasn't a vacation, merely a diversion in work. Alice, the cook, was in high spirits and good humor, seeing that all were fed. She enjoyed the display of her culinary art and the praise that was forthcoming. Reindeer steaks were cheap, so there was great ado in our house with teas, dinners, and a social good time; all this old-fashioned merrymaking was good for morale.

Our log schoolhouse was the headquarters of the reindeer herders and served many other purposes besides; one of the

Winners of a contest at the Reindeer Fair, Akiak.
(Photograph by John Felder.
Courtesy of the Yugtarvik Regional Museum, Bethel, Alaska.)

two rooms displayed the many gifts that had been contributed by the various traders on the river—gifts to be awarded as prizes to the winners, both men and women, at the close of the fair. The other room, which was much larger, was used as the scene of the courtroom sessions each evening, and at other times it was the social center for stag parties and bull sessions. It was also the sleeping quarters for any of the white men who wished to place their sleeping bags on the floor for a night's lodging, a sort of flophouse.

One of the overnight visitors was the target for much fun and laughter; he was accused of being greatly in love or a pantywaist; in his possession was a pair of gaily colored silk pajamas, the like of which was unheard of as being worn by a real he-man on the trail.

The natives never needed to worry as to whether they would find reservations or a place to sleep, for the kashgee was always open to travelers—a warm shelter from the cold.

The events for each day had all been previously arranged by

the leaders, and everything proceeded according to schedule; not even the weather interfered.

A happy crowd had gathered in the village, and red-cheeked, full-faced Eskimos went about smiling. It was a chance for some to be back with their families. They are a home-loving people.

There were no gates or entrance fees to the races, no amphitheaters as we moved around to keep warm, no playlands, carnivals, exhibitions of merchandise, clowns, or clown stunts performed at this fair, for it was different and unique in its character, but it was an interesting show in God's great out-of-doors.

The reindeer herders were definitely the cream of the race and a splendid type of young men, for only those with vim, vigor, and vitality stuck to the three years of training. The lazier ones returned to the village after the first trial to lie around the town and fish when they were hungry.

The United States government herds were supervised by men appointed by Uncle Sam. Under these men, apprentices were in training for a period of three years. During this time of service, they were provided with shelter, some food, and clothing. The shelter was a tent with a camp stove; the food was just essential staples, like sugar, beans, flour, and rice; and the clothing was socks, pants, shirts, rubber boots, and raincoats. In addition to this supply, they were awarded three female deer at the end of the year, that is, if they were deserving. This was the beginning of their own private herd, which would grow during their apprenticeship. They were not permitted to dispose of the females, but the males were butchered for food or sold, as the owner wished.

One roguish apprentice often found female deer in the government herd with a broken leg or injured to such an extent that it was necessary to have it killed for meat. Finally, too many animals were rendered as cripples, and soon thereafter this scalawag was discovered to be a wolf in sheep's clothing with a decided appetite for reindeer steaks. He thoroughly enjoyed the life of a herder, being the ringleader of the many apprentices; but he was obliged to forfeit this pleasure for a year as a penalty for having injured the deer.

The first event on the calendar of the week's program was target shooting, and anyone who wished could participate in this sport. The children had made a hundred of these bull's-eyes of gay colors in the schoolroom.

In the second contest the participants were given a certain length of time to butcher a deer and then carve it into the special cuts, but only two men took part in this race. I didn't witness this gruesome performance. As a girl I had visited the stockyards as a part of my education—which part I really don't know—but the hogs were quickly ducked in cold water by one man; then another person slashed their throats; and still another man skinned them; and so on down the line until every part of the hog was dressed, and the waste turned into fertilizer. For days after this ghastly sight, fish was on my menu. Once in a lifetime is too often to attend an exhibition of that sort.

To come back to the fair, besides these contests there were four reindeer races, which were thrilling to watch. In the first race each of three men lassoed his own unbroken sled deer, harnessed him, hitched him to a sled, and then attempted to drive the furiously bucking animal for the distance of half a mile. This was wild and exciting, taking much time, but eventually, after practically wearing the deer down, the race was won.

The contest was held in a lagoon with a background of trees. I had selected my tree before the race got underway, so I could dash for security if the occasion demanded safety, but after all it wasn't necessary, for the deer seemed to steer away from the sidelines. When the races were in progress, it was my inclination to yell, whoop, and cheer the winners, the same as we did at football games, but the natives stood in mute silence.

The second race was open to all who wished to enter. In this contest numerous sticks or light poles had been placed in the snow at certain intervals on the wide open spaces of the river. All the actors in this game drove their deer attached to a sled in and out among these sticks to see who could pick up the greatest number in a given amount of time.

In the third contest each man lashed his sled, attached his deer, and then drove off at the shot of a gun around a circle nearly a mile in distance. Each of the men taking part in this act must completely upset his sled three times before he returned to the starting point. The one who made the home run first, with everything remaining as snugly intact as when he took off, was the winner.

The longest competition was a race—the distance of three miles. In this rivalry they drove down the main channel of the river, circled an island, and then returned to the starting point.

One Beau Brummel with a devil-may-care attitude was handed the blue ribbon for his great feat in making the run in so short a time, and this he proudly accepted; one of the other men reluctantly took the second prize. Nothing at that time was said about the fairness of the award, but that evening in the courtroom two losing participants very strongly objected to the decision of the judges.

They made the complaint that the driver who had led the way home so triumphantly, and who had so gallantly accepted the laurels, had completely lost control of his deer as they circled the island, thereby endangering their lives, and that in their opinion he was most definitely not worthy of the honor bestowed upon him.

In this trial the winner not only lost his blue ribbon, but he was most severely reprimanded for his dishonor. His glory turned to shame quickly, and he looked as if he were going to cry as he hid his face in humiliation. It wasn't that he cared that he had pulled such a prank, but rather, that his caprice behind the scenes was bared to the public.

At the close of the fair, prizes were awarded for the best workmanship of all the articles made of fur by the wives of the herders. These articles included, principally, parkas, fur caps, mittens, moccasins, and mukluks. These ladies were also presented with gifts for their exquisite beadwork on various exhibits.

The lady who remained with her husband in camp the longest period of the year was also remembered with awards, but on the other hand, mothers with children of school age were not supposed to remain in camp during the winter.

The best harness and sleds were also given recognition. Skis and snowshoes, too, were on the competition list.

The reindeer courts with appointed judges and other needed officers were most interesting and decidedly necessary to the life of the reindeer industry if it were to function with any semblance of law and order. There were many problems that confronted the men involved in the camps from day to day. The herders were summoned to appear in court when their grievances were given hearing, and many difficulties were resolved at this assembly. One government employee, whose dog team had injured a native's reindeer on the highway, was asked to pay the damages sustained in the accident—dogs and reindeer have equal rights on the roadways. One herder had left his dogs shut up for three days in his cabin without food and water while he went on a pleasure trip. For this offense he was obliged to forfeit three months' pay. He wept salty tears.

Records of all the proceedings are kept in the government files. Also, each animal is branded, but unlike our cattle, the ears are clipped with a mark resembling an insect, perhaps a fly, a bee, or a wasp. Each herder has his distinctive cut, so the deer can easily be claimed by the rightful owner.

When the prizes were awarded, and the court sessions over, the fair ended and all returned to their respective ways of living in a happy frame of mind, except for perhaps a few of the herders who felt that the penalties which they had been asked to pay were a bit too exacting.

CHAPTER 12

A Potlatch

Shortly after the holidays, two of the older boys were absent from school. When the roll was called for the day, I asked the children, "Where is Willie Jackson? Where is Johnnie Owens?" No one answered. They acted guilty, but at the same time, they sat in their seats glancing at each other. At last one little boy dared to talk, but then the others looked daggers at him and frowned unmercifully. Finally he said, "I am bashful to look at the sun." The sun was shining in his seat, but he had cleverly changed the subject, fearing to let the cat out of the bag. As a last resort, I told them they didn't need to work. They could put their things away and sit very quietly until the spirit moved them to answer my question. This silence lasted a very few minutes, when one little fellow, who was braver than the rest, offered the desired information in his broken English while the others gave him a dirty look.

"Him go with him papa to Quichluk. Tonight we dance. Last night him go with him papa up the river to invite village. Big time tonight, plenty dance."

A little later in the day, dog team after dog team came bounding up the frozen riverbank and into the village for that night's party; moreover, the air was electric with excitement, for every team that dashed into the village caused the children to stand on their feet to stare out of the window. The naughty rascals had never before behaved in this fashion. They might as well have gone home for the day, since their minds were anywhere but on their books.

Most of these gay and happy visitors had friends in the village who had previously issued them an invitation to be their guests for this gala occasion, but those who had no other shelter occupied the council hall, the kashgee, which was always open to travelers.

This kashgee was built on the same plan as an igloo, but it was different in three respects: it was made on a much larger scale and was a rotunda in shape; then, in addition, the center was a sunken pit. This community hall could be the answer to many needs, for it served the purpose of a hotel, a workshop, a bathhouse, and a social center. In the kashgee men worked on their sleds or boats, oiled and mended the dog harness, and did whatever the occasion demanded, since here they kept their own homes from being littered with debris.

The center of this sunken dwelling was sometimes paved with stone, and here the men enjoyed their steam baths, afterward going out in the snow to roll in the nude; however, I couldn't offer substantial proof to this last performance, for I was never an eyewitness. This unique way of bathing answered in a primitive way the same purpose as our hot and cold shower.

The dances, which were a happy festival to them, were held in this roomy underground auditorium.

My girlfriends of the portage, who lived across the river, came over to enjoy this convivial event with me, for we wanted to witness this potlatch dance, at least on this our first occasion.

The couples danced on the edge of the pit to the weird music of a homemade drum while the natives on the sidelines kept time to melody in an uncanny chant. The dancers moved from side to side on their toes with their hands on their hips, but always remaining in the same spot. They moved with surprising grace and rapidity and in perfect rhythm, and as they danced the lady looked down in a coy, bashful way. It was, indeed, a simple, artless dance. The light was never dimmed, and they never touched each other throughout the performance.

When these one or two couples were exhausted, others took their places, and the dance went on and on without the floor space ever being crowded—only occasionally did they resort to the objectionable in their sign language or gestures.

When the dance was over, the potlatch began, and this was continued until the early morning hours, for there were many gifts to be distributed: yards and yards of fabric were unwrapped from the bolts and then exhibited around the room. In fact, each one present attempted to outdo the others in the length of this material; besides, gifts of most everything imaginable were presented—large and small, cheap and costly—and things unheard of were bestowed on the visiting friends. The oldest guests at this assemblage were showered with the greatest amount of gifts, while the very young were scarcely remembered. The host, who had donated the most generously at this dance, was the "big shot" of the party.

The next morning one man called Black Nick was demolishing one room of his two-room cabin, and as I passed by very early I asked him why he was performing such a rash act as to wreck his home in the middle of winter. To my surprise, he replied proudly and as if it were a feather in his cap, "I dance him away last night." This seemed a very inane action on his part, but he had apartments to let in more ways than one.

One village down on the coast near Nelson Island held a dance for the neighboring colony, and at this dance they even forfeited their dog teams. The beluga, or white whale, are their main source of subsistence; hence, when these animals of the sea arrive in the bay, the Eskimos congregate in large numbers to herd them into shallow waters, where they are corralled and left stranded until the tide goes out. Then they are immediately butchered for food, for especially do they relish the oil. As a result of all their folly, those who gave away their dog teams were without conveyance to the coast, and most of the village starved.

Both the missions and the schools have put forth a great effort to show the natives the sheer foolishness of these rash acts, but it is an inbred custom that is most difficult to change with the old-timers.

The next day at school was most dull and tiresome because both the teacher and the pupils were badly in need of sleep.

CHAPTER 13

Trip to a Reindeer Camp

Six months had passed since my arrival in the little village, and not once had I been off duty except to visit the two girls across the river who had come into the country with me. Since a person becomes very much on edge being shut in all winter, my superiors went into a huddle as to how, where, and when a change of scenery might add a little zest to my routine life. Where to go was a puzzling question; dog team, reindeer, or snowshoes were the only means of transportation, and places for relaxation were few in weather bordering on sixty below. My vacation had to be on a weekend, for I was a schoolteacher with no available substitute, and schools in Alaska were kept in session just as strictly as they were in the States. The problem was finally solved when my supervisors learned that two good-natured, red-faced, and seasoned Eskimo reindeer men were leaving at dawn on Saturday morning for a short day's journey to a reindeer camp. All arrangements could be made for me to travel with these two genial hosts if I wished to accept their hospitality. The prospect was beyond my wildest dreams of a vacation.

I quickly and easily decided what to wear. There was only one sensible costume to be selected if my bones were not to be chilled to the marrow. Money wasn't needed, and my teeth could go unbrushed for the time being. The cold and the place required me to sleep in my clothes—the task of holding on to myself would be a big undertaking without thinking of baggage. The wearing apparel weighed me down but was typical Alaska style for the northern highway in midwinter and the very finest that the country had to offer. The first layer was a pair of long underwear, which gave me a slight tinge of nostalgia for my girlhood days on the prairies. Over this first layer went a heavy woolen khaki shirt and a pair of woolen equestrian trousers. My feet were protected with three pairs of men's heavy woolen socks and a pair of fur boots, called mukluks. The tops of these boots were made of caribou skin, with soles of leather neatly shaped by the older women, whose teeth were worn to the quick in the art of boot making; then, in addition to all this, tundra grass, shaped into soles, was placed inside the mukluks to absorb the dampness from the ground.

My fur coat was a parka, fashioned like an elongated shirt and made of a hundred or more gray squirrel skins; there was an unpleasant, choking, tight squeeze when it was slipped over the head, but with no front opening it kept out the cold and the wind. The hood to his garment was edged with a narrow strip of wolverine to shelter the face from wind and snow. This tiny ruffle was more expensive than the price of a good hat, but it had the quality of keeping dry in damp weather; and under this hood, which was attached to the parka, was worn a beautiful beaver-skin cap—my pride and joy. All this fur rigging was trimmed with tassels of colored yarn, and, among the Eskimos, the younger the wearer the more tassels. These were graduated until the very old were without decorations, so one's years were marked by the amount of ornaments. Mine didn't have too much beauty. To top all this was a *cushbrook* made of denim fabric that served the purpose of a raincoat. It was shaped like the parka and worn over it. My fur mittens of rabbit skins were attached to a cord of colored yarn, like those I wore as a child to keep them safe. Tied in this manner, they were easily slipped off and on in the cold.

My sleeping bag for the night was the last, but not the least, of my requirements on this outing. The fur of the reindeer skins was placed inside with a covering of denim on the outside, a fabric much like the material on a bed mattress. The slit in this bag, down the middle in the upper part, was of sufficient length for me to slip into with ease. A lap of fur was attached to this opening, and it was fastened with snaps and buckles like those on my riding bridle, so that only my nose was exposed to the cold when necessary for breathing. It was often red.

This huge bag was not only airtight, but also watertight, for on one occasion I had taken the hot-water bottle to bed with me and for some reason the cork came out. What a miserable mess it was before the bed was finally dry enough for use again. It was necessary to turn the bag inside out to empty the water and dry the fur, and after that it was almost impossible to turn it back into shape.

I woke early that Saturday morning in a state of great happiness. Everything was ready. A white deer with graceful antlers was at the door attached to a sled. Two Eskimo herders dressed in their fur regalia with happy, smiling red faces were waiting to be gone. Perhaps they were smiling because I was to join them on this unusual drive; it was going to be a hard, cold trip but I would go if it killed me.

We were soon speeding on the way out of town with all the dogs yelping at their chains' length and some of the huskies letting out a melancholy wail. It wouldn't have taken these beautiful but mean and vicious dogs any time to destroy my helpless animal if their chains had broken; hence it was satisfying to be out of their hearing and on the river trail with its wide open spaces where all was peace and quiet save the crunching of the snow and ice under the sled. My deer didn't travel with any of the graces of Dasher, Dancer, Prancer,

Vixen, or Blitzen, for he was somewhat of a clumsy brute, having been used as a freighting animal.

All went well on the open river, but when we entered the portage where the way led out through the beautiful evergreen trees, the devil asked for his dues, and he did it quickly. My sled hit the first tree with a bang, and the deer was instantly separated from the sled—a poor beginning. The guides must have anticipated this accident, since I hadn't learned the art of guiding my sled in and out among the trees; they quickly and good-naturedly came to my rescue, saying, "We not worry. We fixum." The damage caused by this sudden impact was slight, thank goodness, so the animal was soon reattached to the runners and we were again on the way. I had quickly to master the knack of maneuvering my sled this way and that to avoid a second wreck and much embarrassment, for there were many portages ahead to be crossed; they might have asked me to forfeit driving my deer and ride with them. It would have been a humiliating and keen disappointment not to master the situation. I had to tend strictly to business.

On the second portage I managed under difficulty and with much fear and trembling to reach the lagoon without hitting another tree, so my hopes brightened; but here again the old devil was asking for trouble. Suddenly we came upon a dog team that instantly became unmanageable, setting out at a rapid pace to prey upon my beast; he, timid and defenseless, at once whirled around, dashing into the tall timber for safety, catching his antlers in the branches of a tree, and snapping them off before I could realize what was happening—it was shedding time, but much of the romance was gone in driving a hornless animal. In the meantime the yelping, bloodthirsty malamutes, who always ferociously forced traffic to pull aside for them, were brought under control by their driver, and the highway was safe once more from their sharp fangs.

We crossed many portages and lagoons, but finally left them behind with no more trees on the route to keep me in suspense.

We traveled over hill, valley, and desolate snow plains that were alluring and fascinating. There wasn't much animal life to be seen, for the weather was too severe for animals to venture out on their playgrounds. The hare, the fox, and the wolves were the only creatures that could withstand the cold. One lone fox was seen on the edge of the forest, skirting in and out among the trees. There were no wolves in view, but an occasional rabbit scampered from its burrow, sitting upon its haunches to see what was taking place in his remote world. The white ptarmigan, aroused by our coming, flew from tree to tree, and if Alice had been along she would have wanted to set snares to catch these birds, for their fat breasts were a delicacy; but I didn't know the ways and means of capturing them. Neither could I lay low a fox or a rabbit. I didn't have a gun, and killing was no pleasure for me.

Most of the time I sat on my sled for the obvious reason that my many layers of clothing were too bunglesome and weighty for running; however, when my blood began to run cold, since no amount of clothing could keep me warm, I held on to the handles, trotting along behind, but this was only for short intervals.

It grew monotonous following the guides so I thoughtlessly steered my deer around the other two animals and was very soon in the lead. In Kansas I had enjoyed both riding and driving a horse, and this would be a fine chance to demonstrate my ability as a driver—but reindeer like traveling together. As a result, my lead was of very short duration, for in the twinkling of an eye he whirled around to join his comrades; once he had started on his mad career nothing would stop him except throwing him with a rope, and that I couldn't do. My sled upset, tangling me in the lasso rope that had been given me for lines. Somehow I managed to rid myself of the sled and ropes, and he came to a halt when he was back with his companions. A trained deer will stop if the rope is pulled until his head is turned, but my lesson hadn't gotten that far. I suffered no bodily harm, save a few black and blue places, but my pride and feelings were badly hurt for having pulled such a silly prank.

That was the third mishap, and since the third is supposed to be the charm, my superstitious mind was at ease. All these delays caused the morning to pass quickly, but the afternoon seemed long with the shadows now beginning to lengthen and the wind blowing a slight gale.

I kept looking for chimney smoke. Surely around the next bend or over the hill something would be visible in the near distance, but we continued on our way, getting colder and colder, as the day advanced. Finally—a wonderful sight, too enchanting to be a reality—a fabulous fairyland could be seen on the hillside—a thousand reindeer in one herd, digging under the snow for moss.[11] Not far away a stream of smokelike vapor poured into the sky from a mound-shaped igloo. This resembled a house on fire, as the smoke whirled and swirled, lifting itself upward into the air, but it was a most welcome sight. It reminded me of my childhood days when we accompanied our parents in a spring wagon across the country on the yearly midwinter pilgrimage to pay the taxes and buy winter clothing. Then we had a bag of hot salt or bricks to keep our feet warm, but long before we reached our destination, our souls were warmed by smoke from the railroad roundhouse.

This igloo represented a very crude construction for a home, but it answered all the needs of the reindeer herders and their families, and moreover it provided a junction roadhouse for travelers. It resembled somewhat our root cellar on the farm, yet it was quite different, for it had one window in the ceiling and the entrance was more devious. A hole or a pit for the one room, sixteen by twenty feet, had been dug to the depth of six feet, and these walls were lined with wide, rough boards; its floor, too, was covered with the same material. Logs had been placed slopingly on the roof, and all this area was then covered with a thick layer of dirt, except for a small space in the center; over this opening was stretched the bladder of a bear, which served the purpose of a window for light and sunshine.

The entrance to this abode, definitely crude and cramped, making it difficult to get in, was a tunnel about eight feet in length with just space enough to crawl through to the main entrance. The tight squeeze would have been filthy, but the weather was too cold to leave the ground wet. At the entrance proper hung a bearskin to keep out the cold. This door was raised two feet above the floor, making it necessary to step down to enter. There was no sign, "Watch your step," so I stumbled headlong into the place, partly from mere awkwardness, but mostly because my eyes were blinded from the glare of the sun on the trail.

The three Eskimo herders' wives were surprised to see me, but they were smiling and cordial in their welcome. One immediately served hot tea and the pilot bread; the other two kept on with their sewing of furs.

To my surprise and pleasure this igloo was neat and clean, for Eskimo ladies sweep their homes with the mere wing of a wild goose, which is a most unique way of reaching all the corners; the only hardship in this novel way of cleaning is squatting on the floor, but they are accustomed to that sort of life.

In the rear of this hovel was a camp stove with wood piled high and neatly against the wall. Reindeer apprentices kept this fuel well in stock for the winter, with cords and cords in reserve nearby.

Each lady had her own sewing kit and grub box. The box was quite similar to our picnic outfits, but both containers were kept in perfect order; they had few tools to do their work, but they were supplied with the essentials, which were sweet simplicity to them.

On each side of the igloo were raised platforms with a side board that served the purpose of beds. In this home were four, two on each side of the room, and each lady sat on her own bunk as she sewed and worked in the daytime.

There was no consideration for privacy in their building plan. I slept in my clothes and the "privy" was a blade of grass or any protection on the outside that might serve for shelter. One little boy went out into the open to answer nature's call, and I looked at him in hopes of putting him to shame for this public act; surprisingly, he came over in disgust to where I was standing and said in no uncertain terms, "Schoolteacher, why you look?" This reprimand was definitely coming to me.

When we arrived that evening, our appetites were craving food, for we had been six hours on the way without a morsel. I wondered what would be on the dinner menu! Perhaps black-fish from the lakes of the tundra! They are delicious, but to my surprise one of the ladies dressed an arctic hare for this meal. After she had stewed the meat for some time in water melted from snow, rice was added. Never was my hunger more violent or food more delicious.

It had been my plan to sleep in my bag on the sled in a sheltered place outside, but the weather was much too severe; when one's breath freezes it's sensible to remain under cover. For this reason I gladly accepted the invitation to cast my lot with theirs and place my bag on the floor between the bunks. It was a hard bed, but nothing is more conducive to sleep than exhaustion from a long day of travel in the wind and cold, and I was very tired.

During the night my hair grew wet; I thought that the snow had melted and leaked through the bladder-skin window above me, but the bearskin door had been opened directly above the bed, causing an impact of heat and cold, which dampened my long, braided locks.

We had expected severe weather the next day for our home-ward trip, but to our pleasure the temperature had greatly moderated and the cold wind had stopped blowing. Nowhere on the globe does the climate vary as it does in this part of the world. The powerful Chinook winds coming up the Kusko-kwim River can make great changes in the weather in a few hours. I have seen the thermometer register forty below one day, and then climb to forty above the next.

My reservations in this unique lodge had been made for only one night; therefore we departed for home the next morning, making the most of the sunshine and the swiftly shortening day. We exchanged our tired animals for fresh reindeer, so the going was much speedier, and happier for me since this new animal had antlers.

My vacation ended with no mishap on the homeward stretch, but my muscles were sore for days. It takes a rugged individual to withstand the rigors of the trail, but the pleasure of the journey, there and on the way, was well worth the energy expended.

CHAPTER 14

The Kuskokwim River

Tourists who visit Alaska seldom travel far enough west to see the beauties and magnificence of the Kuskokwim River. It is the second largest river in Alaska, with its headwaters in the many unexplored regions of the majestic Alaskan range. All the small, rushing, leaping streams unite in power to provide a water basin of 50,000 square miles, and it affords 800 miles of navigation for various kinds of watercraft. Oceangoing vessels navigate to Bethel, river steamers churn the waters to McGrath, and graduated sizes of canoes and kayaks sail on the narrow, shallow streams that are little more than babbling brooks.

The waters of the South, East, and North Forks together with the Takotna River unite and combine to form the Kuskokwim proper. Here it gains in momentum and power, mile by mile, as it is fed by the melting snow and ice, flowing through the many unseen canyons to the great ocean. The Swift, the Stony, the Hoholitna, Crooked Creek, and Tuluksak, with untold and unnamed sloughs, flow from all points of the compass to help swell its magnitude. The mouth of the river, where it enters into the Bering Sea, is a great source of worry to most navigators. The river channel is forever changing. The mud flats spread out in low water as far as the eye can see. Sailors travel on half-tides. The low tides are too shallow and the high tides might leave them stranded on mudflats as the water reaches low ebb.

This awe-inspiring river has little recorded history since it is so isolated and inaccessible. It is practically unknown, compared with the much-written-about river Jordan, so inextricably interwoven with human life. Its history and its people are just coming to the front; in fact, many outside of Alaska have never heard of the word "Kuskokwim," meaning "cough river," "Kus" (cough) "kwim" (river).

This fast-moving stream sparkles on its way, animated and endowed with a fighting spirit; it twists and turns, whirls and leaps, burrows and squirms, both sides seeking madly to reach a goal. It has never been dammed or spanned; it stops for no umpire. It just keeps moving along as we do in life, intent on winning.

The Kuskokwim River not only gives pleasure and beauty, but bloodcurdling tales are told of its treachery and devouring terror. Dog teams and driver have plunged headlong through the ice to a watery, unknown grave; skaters at a gay and merry party have rushed heedlessly into unexpected air holes and been hopelessly lost under the ice; men in heavy trucks have crashed into the cold, deep water, tragically pinioned with no human means of escape; boats have been carried swiftly downward with all lost in the river's might and power.

The freeze-up was interesting, but it was quite different from what my geography led me to believe. The old river never waited until we were ready; year in and year out it had a task to perform. We might be caught far from home or with the boat held in its icy fangs. When nature set the time, it began blanketing itself with a lusty layer of ice, sometimes thinner and sometimes thicker, as the universe demanded. It made its own hibernal covering in much the same fashion as we would piece together a crazy quilt. The myriads of blocks of various shapes and sizes of one glistening color were so firmly integrated that only through the mighty power of old Sol could they be torn asunder.

A swift stream with whirlpools and powerful currents does not usually freeze over in just one night like a calm and tranquil lake; to begin with, the mighty Kuskokwim starts its refrigeration along the edges and then each day and night reaches out into the stream. When the action of the strong current breaks the ice loose from its moorings, it then floats downward toward the sea, joining to other broken parts. This process continues until the entire mass is consolidated and the river is firmly tucked in from bank to bank with its winter wrap. The days covered in this operation depend on the state of the weather and how quickly it acts to accomplish this enormous task. The ice now freezes thicker and deeper until it is safe for travelers—a seasonal highway that lasts for at least six months.

There is no temporizing with the weather either in the fall or spring; when the snow and ice in the many tributaries begin to melt, the water in the main river rises. This inundation lifts the ice, breaking the shore clasps loose from their anchor and leaving the whole mass free to follow the current. In its destructive and devouring momentum the ice is jammed and crushed into smaller pieces, producing a terrific thunderlike noise as it fights its way ruthlessly onward to the sea. In its mighty and mad force it works like an excavator, digging up the spruce and willow trees, shaving and gouging into the banks along the way, ever changing the bed of the river.

As the ice drifted by in a glamorous, lively parade, our imaginations pictured all kinds of sights on this fast-moving body. We fancied seeing men and their dog teams, cabins, animal life, and property of all kinds caught in the dangerous, monstrous, turbulent flow of ice and water; but our field glasses soon allayed our fears and put our minds at rest. It was only debris collected along the way.

The ice jammed our station, causing extreme high water for

one day, and as a result we had a jolly good time sailing around the village in boats while it lasted. The government house and the church were the only spots high enough to escape the rip-roaring deluge. A boat was anchored at each door for emergency. During this time, we were packed with refugees for the night almost as tight as in our camp on the portage. Huge cakes of ice floated through the main street, and when the water suddenly dropped, these mammoth icebergs were left at our front doors to melt—a refrigeration that lasted for several days.

The Kuskokwim, a mellifluous name, flows through a very rich country, rich in various kinds of minerals, in many kinds of fish, in animal life, in grass and flowers, rich in beauty, a wonderful playland to those who love nature and the great God-given out-of-doors.

CHAPTER 15

Making a Garden

The seasons of Alaska were most interesting, and each period ushered in a new round of work and pleasure. Winter had brought the dances and the Reindeer Fair, and, before we were conscious of the march of time, spring had arrived with its garden activities.

My knowledge of the scientific cultivation of the soil was limited, but since a teacher must be many-sided in her duties in a frontier country, it was essential for me to go to work in earnest to learn the ways of farming under different climatic conditions—especially if there was to be a harvest.[12]

Gardening in that country was carried out in a different manner from the way it's done in the States and under difficulties even if time is taken by the forelock. To begin with, the dirt for next year's planting had to be placed in boxes and stored in the root cellar early in the fall to keep it from freezing. There could be no sowing if we didn't steal a march on the weather, for the earth was frozen and impervious to garden tools in the wintertime. It was equally important to have seeds purchased well in advance, for often it was necessary to send to the States for the supply.

Some people were fortunate enough to own their own greenhouses, but our huge kitchen served that purpose for us.

It was light, warm, and spacious, with one side completely framed by windows.

The boxes, filled with earth, were carted from the cellar in March and placed on racks in front of the windows for the contents to be thoroughly warmed; after this, it was thrilling to pulverize the soil with bare hands, but more wonderful to observe the little sprouts bursting forth into green plants when all around the ground was barren and black.

The seeds were at first scattered quite close together to sprout and develop into tiny-sized plants before transplanting them to other containers, where they were later placed further apart. Cabbage, head lettuce, and cauliflower grew luxuriously, making it imperative that they be reset in other boxes two or three times before the out-of-doors garden was sufficiently warm not to retard the growth.

Potatoes, cut with an eye in each part, were carefully placed in the cartons filled with humus until the leaves began to flourish; then they were replanted in the garden very painstakingly with the foliage above the soil. This gave them a head start, and they were well on the way to maturity with little delay. We also grew Petroski turnips, called the Alaska apple because they are delicious.

Since the growing season was so short, the whole secret of success was to have every vegetable expanding and ready to set in the ground the instant the ice left the river. Summer had then arrived, with no more frost until late in August. Because there was almost perpetual sunlight for twenty-four hours each day during the summer, vegetables—growing in so much light— are crisper and tastier than those in the States.

When the navigation season opened and the fish began to run, all the people of the village hurriedly departed for the fishing grounds, leaving the town deserted. Even the halt, the lame, and the blind were transported to tent life in the sunshine and fresh air and to get a serving of the season's first king salmon. Making a garden and directing the school greenhouses were a part of the way I earned my summer salary, but when the fish arrived, the children abandoned their hotbeds for the fish camps; however, it was necessary for them to accompany their parents, for fish was their main food during the entire year and vegetables were not much to their liking. Those who raised potatoes sold most of their yield to the trader.

There wasn't a soul left in the village to spade my tiny truck farm. The plants were ready, but no ground was prepared. Something had to be done about the cultivation immediately or there would be no fresh vegetables. Having all the necessary tools for gardening on hand, I thought I might as well spade a little each day as to sit and fret, so I went to work with the spade. When the superintendent, Mr. Kilbuck, arrived my spading was completed, and I expected that some praise would be forthcoming for manual labor accomplished with so much sweat, muscle, and happiness, but it wasn't. Instead, he said in his quiet and reserved manner, "It looks well tilled on the top, but the ground underneath hasn't been spaded very deeply."

Well, I seemed to be up against a stone wall, even though my plans had been most thoroughly organized, but as usual, I was never fenced in without some unexpected means of escape. This time it was a deaf-mute from up the river who came to my rescue. This Eskimo had arrived in our village for the summer, hoping to find odd jobs, and he would dig deep into the earth.

He had with him all his meager possessions for a home and light housekeeping—the Eskimo summer way of life. In a short time he had erected his tent near the river, where he was comfortably housed, and was eager to work. He was a smiling, happy soul in this thirties, and very religious, so much so that he named his canvas shelter Jesus. The letters were in large-sized capitals, framed across the top of his tent, so they could be seen across the village. Just why a camp should be called this sacred name was never disclosed, for my sign language didn't develop to the point where I could converse with him in his Eskimo vernacular.

It was evident that this was the first time he had ever worked in a garden. While he was, indeed, a good spader, I was annoyed to the point of tears when he began to dig up the potatoes and leave the weeds growing in carefully tended rows.

To work outside in the fresh, balmy air and sunshine after being shut in all winter, and to see nature's breath of life performing miracles, was a great source of enjoyment—until the pesky mosquitoes arrived. Having them hatch and ready to sting almost before the frost was out of the air was most provoking. The north country would be a paradise in summer if these tiny ubiquitous insects were not on hand, posthaste, to torment night and day.

It was evident that I could do nothing without some sort of protection, so I took time out to prepare the customary armor for battle. I protected my face with a black mosquito net, which was made into an elongated bag with elastic inserted in both ends. One end was securely fastened around the crown of a broad-brimmed hat, and this held the net away from my face; the other end was stretched over my shoulders and then fastened securely with straps under my arms. With this functional millinery on my head, gloves on my hands, and a pair of equestrian trousers, I returned to the garden to defy my foes; but if one or two found the way beneath this fortress, they speedily sent me back for better protection. The first year their sting seemed to inoculate one with poison, for the second year the bites were not as noticeable or the bumps as large.

Making a garden required much thought and labor, but it also provided joy in the doing, with a harvest of vegetables as a final goal. These were then stored in the root cellar, where most of the vegetables kept their firmness without becoming woody or pithy until February. The potatoes were excellent in texture and not the watery sort that grew in some localities. The season was too short for the peas to ripen, since they were not in the ground in time, but we ate them, pods and all, on our various trips to the garden, for they were so good.

While the garden was growing, there was much in the country to gather for food; wild rhubarb, which flourished along the riverbank, was much tastier and sweeter than the domesticated variety. Each one of the homes was provided with the domesticated kind, but the natives didn't like the taste, so they gave me permission to cut some of their supply when they left for the camps. We gathered blueberries, a dish coveted by all Alaskans, which can be served in many different ways (the canned juice is delicious); the low-bush cranberries, which, stored ouside to freeze, remain fresh all winter without the work of canning; and the pale salmonberries, which make an appetizing dessert when preserved with oranges.

In the spring the smelt were the first fish to arrive. The native ladies taught me how to weave a net, which was attached to a wire ring about two feet in diameter, and then to this ring was fastened a long, slim pole for a handle. My catch in dipping for these tiny, silvery creatures wasn't anything to boast about, but there was much joy in the attempt, and the pleasure of rowing was part of the sport. Herring followed the smelt, and the king salmon then trailed the herring—their food. The silver and dog salmon later came in hordes, and in the winter the natives cut a hole in the ice to trap eels for the livers, which they relished.

The ducks and the geese were fat as they began their fall flight to the south, but the government prohibited whites from bringing down the geese for food.

Every Carnation milk can that was opened was thoroughly washed and stored away for future canning use. As the one can was punctured in the opening, it took two to make a whole can in canning; we used these tins in canning salmon. We had no oil paper to line them, but we managed to make our own supply by oiling wrapping paper. We possessed a canning and soldering outfit that was hard to manipulate, but the nurse, who was most capable and ambitious, soldered the cans. In the early morning, we would purchase a forty-pound king salmon, which a native lady quickly skinned with more art and ease than I could skin a cottontail. She removed the bones while we worked fast and furiously to have it sealed in the cans before it spoiled; besides, if a can sent bubbles to the top in cooking, it had to be resealed. Our shelves, after much long and tedious labor, were filled with food.

Reindeer meat was plentiful throughout the winter, though it wasn't supplied in the summer for lack of refrigeration, save on rare occasions when a carcass was brought down from the mountain herds; but then the deep, swift mountain rivers were dangerous to navigate. Rabbits were plentiful, moose could be had, cub bear meat was delicious, and we once roasted a porcupine that tasted like savory roast pork; we also cooked a swan and a loon—the swan was good, but the loon was much too gamey. A lake provided fresh clams, though they were most difficult to raise from the depths of the bed.

Each Eskimo home was provided with a cache, both in the village and in their summer camp. These storehouses were built upon stilts to be safe from the floods and out of reach of stray, hungry dogs; in addition we all had a smokehouse, for both whites and natives relished the smoked salmon strips.

The store of a trader in each village was usually well stocked with all the necessary staple goods, so if one had what it took to glean the harvest, there was food, and food to spare.

CHAPTER 16

Birth of a Baby

Many varied happenings took place that first summer. The ice had come and gone and I passed from the ranks of a cheechako to that of a sourdough. The death of our dog Prince was a solemn occasion. We wept when he was gone; he was so much a part of our lives. On the other hand it was a joyous occasion when Ole Andersen was married, and we were happy and found wanting when Alice was wed for the third time. The birth of Betty Andersen's new baby caused the most excitement. Thus, in three short months the three profound wonders of life—love culminating in marriage, a death, and a birth— took place in our little community.

The springtime was a happy season when the warm sun uncovered the water. The birds made their cheerful return; the ducks of various families and colors playfully plunged in and out of the river; the geese, flock after flock, flew high in the sky, honking and honking to announce their arrival as they went on their way in perfect formation to their usual nesting places in the swamps and tundra; the birds of many species in their gayest plumage flitted from tree to tree, seemingly on their Easter parade. We were delighted to welcome these rich travelers of the air who, judging from the music rendered, were joyful to return to their summer homes.

The salmon, en route to the purly spawning grounds, leapt and played in the river as they found their way to their birthplace.

The furred marten and mink, the sly wolverine, the slinking fox, and the stealthy lynx had more security from the winter trapper; the busy beaver came out to build his dam; the magnificent moose with its wide antlers roamed the woodlands; the graceful caribou feeding on the green were always nervously alerted for the marauding wolves, their inexorable foe; and the lumbering bears, emerging from the winter dens, wandered aimlessly in the sheltering woods.

The land that was oozing like a sponge, with the earth frozen to a depth of three feet even in the summer, was now covered with an exuberant growth of wild grasses. The woodlands modeled their summer robes of many kinds of moss and the fragrant wildflowers were waiting for the sun to uncover their heads; even before the snow is gone they are smiling and nodding in the sunshine.

When the twisting, turning, jamming ice had left the river in three days or more, we were then out on the banks looking for the first boat. This was an exciting time when the mail, held up for the winter, arrived; fresh fruits and vegetables, with a variety of foods that our appetites craved, were delivered, and along with this was our merchandise, ordered sight unseen. Usually the freighters carried unexpected passengers and we were delighted when Emily Andersen walked down the gangplank from the boat.

Ole Andersen was again in the spirit to sing his favorite song, "Norway, Norway, Land of the Midnight Sun." Emily Andersen, by the same family name, was to have been on the *Yukon* when we arrived, but she had been unavoidably detained in Hammerfest, Norway.

That week Emily and Ole were married in the same favorite chapel where the girls had been married, with the same minister, Mr. Kilbuck, officiating. After the ceremony the bridal party dined in our kitchen. The table had been laid for this happy occasion on a huge hardangar tablecloth made by Emily that winter in Hammerfest.

Emily was a typical Norwegian and soon the favorite in the community. With her tools and various arts, she soon turned her cottage into a beautiful house.

Ole Andersen was a miner, who must make the most of a short work season; for that reason they left for the hills soon after the wedding. A honeymoon to be envied. They sailed the majestic Kuskokwim to the mouth of the slough, which then led them upward to the swift, clear mountain streams. The going was hard but beautiful. When they arrived in the mountains, the birds were there, dressed in their gayest plumage, to welcome them with sweet music. Nature had carpeted the earth with fragrant moss, blooming in various colors, and wildflowers adorned the pathway with beauty and color. Certainly a gorgeous background for lovers.

Lohengrin's music had scarcely faded when our spirits were dimmed and saddened by the death of our dog Prince. We were never able to diagnose the real cause of his ailment or to ease his pain, but it was thought that at one time he had swallowed a fish bone, causing an infection. He suffered and in his misery grew thinner and thinner, weaker and weaker, until he finally gave up the brave fight.

He was a loyal friend. We never entered the house after being away that he didn't immediately rise and come padding over to greet us in his affectionate way; it was perhaps just a wag of his tail, a little woof, or a kiss on our hands, but it was a dog's love and devotion bestowed in dignity. He was our door chimes, for whenever a person not of our family approached our home, either day or night, he would announce their coming. Indeed, he was our father protectorate. We buried him in the woods, while his grieving mate, Shep, shared our sadness.

He left a vacant mat and a lost mate, for Shep, who was the only one of her class in the village, wept silently. After he was gone she followed us more closely; we were proud of her companionship, for she was a beautiful collie lady.

Late that summer, much to our surprise, Alice was wooed and won for the third time. We unfortunately lost our efficient co-worker. Her new husband, an attractive Eskimo, was a Moravian helper in the mission church. He was considered a man of means for his nationality. He was the owner of a large herd of reindeer, owned his own home, and had money deposited in an outside bank. He had also been married once before, which should be a valuable asset in avoiding the quicksands and whirlpools of marriage. Above all, Alice's new cottage was the nicest in the village.

Alice was smiling and happy that fall. Often she said, "Me happy—good man." She did start off with all the best intentions in the world of being a good wife, but with all her turning of new, unstained pages, it wasn't lasting—life and love were a struggle. Being good all the time wasn't in her. Her jealous disposition, which was always her undoing, ruffled the calm and serenity of this new home in a very short time.

On several occasions she left him and returned to "me papa's house," but later returned to the fold. She was blessed with an appealing and winsome manner that seemed to melt the heart of her husband.

The last time she took flight, it wasn't so easy to cross the threshold and ease her way back into his good graces. After much difficulty in the attempt, she related a dream to him that had given her great concern. In the dream she had died. St. Peter had refused to grant her admission into heaven unless she returned to her husband as an obedient and faithful wife. He knew that it was only a ruse, but her scheme worked. He gave in to her pleadings; he didn't care to ban her from heaven. He was so honorable.

Again she was cozily restored to her place as a sweet and loving wife, but there was bound to be another eruption. This time it was a bad one. In this fit of temper, she ripped the corner of the inlaid linoleum and set fire to the kitchen curtains and hurled the dishes at her man. In this mad rage she scurried out of the door and back to "me papa's house."

This was the straw that completely broke the camel's back. Little did he care, after this mad episode, if she never entered heaven; he definitely objected to her sharing his cottage ever after. In the course of time he closed his home, seeking peace and contentment from the tantrums of a seemingly wild woman, and departed to enjoy the solitude of the reindeer camp.

After Alice's third marriage had gone on the rocks, she returned to her father's home, but worked for us during the day when needed.

The most precious event was the birth of a dear baby, the first white child to be born in the white village. Betty Andersen, the girl from Michigan who came into the country to wed the miner, was the mother of a fine baby boy. No one guessed that Elizabeth was going to have a baby until the last few weeks; then the ladies gave showers and we all enjoyed a share in preparing the baby clothes. Elizabeth was more excited over the layette than she had been over her trousseau.

The occasion was so very thrilling. Thrilling to me, too, until Mrs. Evans invited me to attend the birth of the child. That set off the explosive fireworks, for out of a clear sky, Mrs. Evans announced the approximate date of birth and in the same breath said, "I am depending on you to be present for moral support, and to assist if necessary. And besides," she added with a snap to her voice, "it might stand you in good stead sometime, to know just exactly what to do when a baby arrives."

Since there was no doctor to take charge of major operations, the worries and responsibilities fell in the lap of the nurse, but nursing was never one of my aptitudes, and I definitely didn't want to begin with this baby case. Before time was taken to consider the pros and cons, or to look at the duty that must be shouldered from her point of view, she had my answer.

"I am not going. Count me out. My contract doesn't call for a side issue like that. I have never asked you to come into the schoolroom! At home people never talked about having babies, let alone ask a girl to witness a mother in the pangs of childbirth. I am not going."

All this time I had been raving, on and on, the nurse hadn't said a word. She shut up like a clam. That was all out of my system, but it didn't make me feel any better. The nurse said no more. Silence was far from golden; it was a depressive dark blue.

She was a lovely nurse with an exceptional mind, most capable and untiring in her efforts, with no limit for her sacrifice for others; no matter how far the distance, how cold the weather, or how tired she might be from caring for the sick, she would always go to those in need. We shared the same house when she was in the village. She was older and wiser, and, too, she had nursed me when I was sick.

The time was near at hand for the birth of the baby; the nurse's kit was packed with everything needed, in readiness; she was always systematic and most efficient in all that she did. She could go into the dispensary in the dark and put her finger on the right bottle, or if she went for medicine she could even tell which two bottles it was between.

No more was said about my going, but the atmosphere was tense; furthermore my conscience was pricking me, and my heart was heavy. Perhaps my attitude was mean and selfish, and going wouldn't cause me any more suffering than being disloyal. Hasty decisions had always been one of my weak points, making me suffer the aftereffects, but this was definitely a thorn in my flesh. I don't know the real reason why I didn't want to go, but I didn't care to be one of the party. Our friendship was approaching the danger zone. She would never ask me again, that I well knew; after that rude refusal, it was necessary for me to break the ice that I had so quickly frozen.

I would go—but not from choice.

We crossed the river in the early evening, and before midnight the baby had arrived. Nature had performed perfectly— a baby boy!

In every step I watched the nurse, as she had requested me to do. Well do I remember sterilizing the cord that tied the lifeline of mother and child. It really turned out to be an unusual, happy experience. Now I wondered why I fought against going with all my soul.

The next few days, it was my pleasure to care for the mother and infant in the daytime while the nurse slept. This was my chance to atone to a certain extent for my shortcomings, and also to win my way back into Mrs. Evans' good grace.

The nurse usually crossed the river in the morning to our house and to her own bed, but this was a strenuous and tiresome trip, fighting the swift current. To strike the opposite shore nearest the village, one must aim for a point well upstream to allow for the speed of the water; otherwise the boat would land much below our home dock. On this particular day she decided to sleep in one of the nearby cabins that wasn't used during the summer. That night she was miserable, itching and itching, in a most uncomfortable state with incessant petty attacks; even her head of long auburn tresses was creepy. To her surprise and chagrin, she had been exposed to body lice. Now it was her turn to subject herself to the cootie shampoo— chloronaphthalene.

She paid the price, but in the true sense of the word she was a sourdough, for she had seen the ice come—and go—and was lousy.

CHAPTER 17

Dr. Lamb Arrives in Akiak

Alice was at home by herself, lady of the house for the day. She loved it there. Her attachment to the government cottage was passionate, since it had been her home for years. Then, the place took on added joy when she was "mistress of all she surveyed."

I asked her if she minded being alone. Often she pretended not to understand, but this time her black eyes sparkled as she stopped chewing her gum long enough to exclaim, "Me happy, plenty happy. Me bake cookies. Me roast the meat."

The nurse would be asleep just outside in the summer tent after a long night on duty. Alice usually opened and closed the doors quietly; she walked stealthily in her moccasins and seldom made kitchen sounds. If she did give the door a violent slam or rattled her dishes, we knew at once that her anger was gathering momentum and the lid would soon come off.

This was to be my last day across the river playing the role of nurse. My first lessons, in folding diapers, burping the baby, and caring for the mother, would end. I had expected it to be a tough assignment, but it was a happy experience. The mother was little care and so appreciative; the baby thrilled me. The tender little life slept and slept, scarcely taking time out for nourishment.

It was nearing evening on this last day. Only one hour to go before the nurse, Mrs. Evans, would come to take over. I looked out across the Kuskokwim River to see if she had left the yonder shore. The wind had whipped the water to a foam and small canoes were being tossed about on the brilliant blue water. The view of the river always lifted my spirits. She wasn't to be seen anywhere, yet it was early.

I turned to be sure everything was finished for the day. The nurse was very exacting. Nothing must be left undone.

At that very minute Mrs. Evans came into the room. A stranger, a young man whose face was alight and gleaming, followed in her footsteps. She was beamingly happy and displayed more of a professional air than usual. Then she turned, introducing me, "Miss Wynne, this is Dr. Lamb, our new doctor." His smile was sweet, with happiness in his eyes, as he greeted me. He pressed my hand—wonderful.

This was a professional call. He followed the nurse to see the mother and her babe. The nurse wanted the assurance that she had done everything that was humanly possible in this obstetrical case. She was most conscientious.

While they were in consultation, I dashed, pell-mell, over to the grocery store to leave an order. We would need something extra special to serve since this new doctor had arrived to join the government family.

The mail carrier, Oscar Samuelson, and Mr. Felder, a trader from Bethel, were in the store.[13] The new doctor had traveled with them from the Yukon, and the three had already been served a dinner by Alice at our house.

The merchant, George Smith, didn't ask me as usual, "What can I sell you today?" Instead, he cleared his throat with a twinkle in his blue eyes and said, "Have you seen the new doctor?" Before I could answer yes, the mail carrier chimed in, "Don't lose your heart to him; he is already engaged." Then the trader went on, "Marriage plans are underway." They were in a devilish mood at my expense.

When I returned to the home, the doctor was ready to cross the river, as the conference was over. As I put on my coat to go with him, he remarked, "You are taller than I pictured you to be." He knew all about me. Those two traveling companions had left nothing unsaid.

We left together. I wished that we didn't need to pick up the groceries at the store. It would be difficult to act natural, even though I assumed an air of blank indifference.

As we skipped down the bank to the river's edge, he took the groceries and slipped his arm through mine—on the banks were people watching. I was excited and flushed with pleasure and decidedly nervous.

Our means of transportation was a light canoe with oars to buck the wild waves that lashed against the boat. The water was choppy, making headway difficult. The doctor took his coat off and the color rose high in his cheeks as he rowed, even though there was a river breeze and a sharp sting in the evening air.

The nurse had always cautioned me to sit perfectly still, scarcely to breathe, when she was rowing. I was always to blame if there was any disruption. She wouldn't trust her life with me at the oars, but I took a sporting chance with her. Now I sat almost petrified, with the river spray slapping me in the face while he labored with difficulty to reach the shore in safety.

That day was as happy as any day that I remember.

We were curious to know the roads, crossroads, and finally the trails that had landed this doctor in western Alaska. He was young—twenty-eight years old—nearly five feet eleven, with blue eyes and light hair brushed to a shine from his noble brow. He was tender, thoughtful, serious in his profession, but gay and warmhearted in his personality. We all liked him. Even Alice wore her new housedress and went about her work with animation and gaiety. She often exclaimed, "Yung-cha-wista (meaning doctor) fine, fine. Me like." Yet, he was lowered in her estimation when he refused to eat fish.

Dr. Frank Lamb was born in Blissfield, Michigan, in 1888. His father died when he was eight years old. As a consequence his mother moved to Detroit, Michigan, with her three children, one son and two daughters, to make their home with her brother. This uncle, Dr. Hal Wyman, owned and operated the emergency hospital in Detroit, and Frank was educated to join his uncle in the practice of medicine. However, this association was short-lived after his training was ended. His uncle died very suddenly. With this change of affairs, Frank went west and on to Alaska, where he spent two years in Nulato before he came to the Kuskokwim region.

He was attractive, capable, and most invincible. It wasn't long after his arrival that his past loves were forgotten, for we had fallen in love. Alice entered into our romance with enthusiasm, but she was shrewd in knowing what went on; each morning she would smile and in her dramatic way exclaim, "Yung-cha-wista plenty love you. Me see, plenty, plenty love. Happy! Happy!"

I had always scoffed at love at first sight, but that very thing happened to me that summer; I was swept off my feet into a new and wonderful life. I had had romances before, but never the like of this. It was thrilling to hear him say, "You were made especially for me." He was extravagant in his love, and it was, indeed, a magic, heavenly world.

Often we spent the evening in the summer den, a huge tent erected over a board floor. It was a cozy retreat with mosquito netting, comfortable chairs, a table for snacks, and a wood fire which snapped and crackled in the camp stove, lighting the room aglow on cool evenings.

The stage was furnished with a perfect setting for our romance. That was a delightful summer on the Kuskokwim. It was the season when nature was most lavish in her decorations. The weather was beautiful, with not a cloud in our skies. We had a launch, the enchanting Kuskokwim River, the moon; and I the man I adored. What more could a girl ask for? Nothing seemed to mar our happiness, not even the mosquitoes.

On our wedding day, the October sun was shining brightly though the days were growing short. The golden leaves that were not already grounded, fanned by a stiff wind, were turning and twisting as they were wafted downward. Ice was freezing in the river. The snow came creeping quickly down the mountains. Eskimos were busy sawing and cording their wood. Winter had arrived.

It was cold outside, but our heaters kept it warm and snug within. The household was abustle and excited. Everything was under control, except my man didn't have a suit of clothes to wear on this his wedding day. His mother, who came into the country for the wedding, had purchased an English tweed suit in Detroit, but when the box was opened she was nonplussed. The long trousers had been replaced with knickers and wraparound gaiters, suitable for the golf links. I thought he looked perfectly charming in them, but his mother, who was very conventional, said most emphatically, "That suit will never do." She thought a minute and then suggested, "Perhaps you can borrow a suit!" That wasn't easy to do, but the wedding couldn't be delayed. He was loaned a gray gabardine suit by a friend who was much plumper and overtopped him by several inches. An uncomfortable, miserable fit.

The girl who was to have been my maid of honor was a teacher from Bethel, Miss Bienerth, a pretty golden-haired girl with captivating brown eyes. She had come to Akiak ahead of time to bake the wedding cake, her specialty, and to finish her gown, which she was making over by a Vogue pattern for the occasion. That day winter descended on the Kuskokwim with wind and snow, and ice came into the river; consequently, she hurried back to her post before the ceremony to escape being marooned away from her school for several weeks.

That day was short. At four o'clock, the hour set for the ceremony, the sun had already slipped behind the mountain, and the sky had changed its color from saffron to a deep blue. The moon had started on its way across the blue sky and lighted the pathway to the church. The frost nipped my nose. I needed my parka, but slipping it on would have mussed my beautiful white crepe de chine wedding dress, a gift from my mother-in-law-to-be, so I put on a fabric coat instead.

All the white people in the community and some of the natives had assembled in the chapel. I missed my parents, but Mr. Kilbuck, who always seemed to understand, had written them a letter in which he said, "I would gladly consent to my own daughter marrying Dr. Lamb." They needed that encouragement to make them happy, too.

As the music of Mendelssohn and Lohengrin faded away, Mr. Kilbuck performed the nuptial service. Here we vowed to love and cherish one another until death do us part.

Immediately following the ceremony a reception was held in our huge kitchen, which was really the nicest part of the house. Refreshments were served and a few enjoyed dancing to the music of a Victrola. The first thing I knew, my husband had disappeared, but soon returned in his own clothes, saying, "Now I feel like myself."

There was no going-away trip for a time. The ice had come into the river. We began our new life in a log cabin.

CHAPTER 18

An Alaska Wedding Journey

We had been married three weeks before the ice in the river froze solid enough for traveling. Now we could enjoy the delayed honeymoon. Mr. and Mrs. Schwalbe, missionaries at Bethel, had previously invited us to be their guests for the weekend—a doctor couldn't spare a longer time from the hospital just for honeymooning.

Everything needed for the journey was made ready the night before. Alice had come over that evening with smoked king salmon strips that she had cured. She knew that was the only kind of fish the doctor would eat. A tidbit, and her good wishes for a pleasant vacation. We had purchased a bundle of dogfish from a native to feed the dogs if they grew tired or if we were unexpectedly delayed.

We rose early that cold November morning, hoping to be on the trail at break of day. A friend across the river had loaned us his team, five beautiful huskies, and one of those woven picture sleds made for light travel—all of this added to our sporting adventure. Ahead of us was the hike of a long, cold mile across the river to the white village, where the dogs were sheltered in their warm houses.

The dogs were lying on their stomachs, hitched and ready to go when we arrived, so we were soon on our way. I had thought my own mother's wedding trip was unique, but ours rivaled hers. She had followed on the heels of the red men when the Middle West was still a part of the frontier. She traveled with my father as far as the railroad extended, and then from there they continued their journey to the homestead in Phillips County, Kansas, with a team of oxen that jogged slowly over the pioneer roads. We were in the last frontier, traveling with a graceful dog team that trotted faster than the lumbering oxen; but that would be only six miles an hour, that is, if the weather were favorable and nothing unexpected happened to hinder our speed.

I sat in the sled, cuddled up in my furs, while my husband stood on the runners, holding on to the handlebars. Here he could quickly step on the brakes if this belligerent team of huskies decided to bound over the trail at will. The sight of another dog team would make them go wild. Brakes were just as essential on sleds as they are on automobiles. These animals could be brutally dangerous; their teeth were sharp and their hides so tough that only by the lash of a chain could they be made to feel any sort of punishment.

Our spirited team went bounding down the way with heads up and bushy tails in the air, when they stopped abruptly, veered around an air hole, and went on. From then on we traveled more slowly and alertly to avoid a catastrophe. When the river has just frozen over, travel is a bit risky and hazardous to one who doesn't know the perils lurking here and there, and also dangerous to the most seasoned driver if he isn't alert each moment for the possibility of spots of lightly frozen ice. It is often days after the freeze-up before these places are safely covered.

Since we were the first to go over the trail, our friends were worried and apprehensive about our day's ride, and furthermore they didn't expect us to reach our destination that day. They told us so. They suggested that we carry camping facilities or wait until a later date when other travelers had first gone over the trail, but our plans had long since been made, and our friends at the end of the line, who had invited us to be their guests, would be disappointed. Since there were no tangible signs of danger we were not to be dismayed. Naturally, we departed in an atmosphere of doubts and hopes, yet gay and happy.

The trail was quite rough, for a stiff wind was blowing; the night before, the river had completely frozen over, and as a result, many frozen bumps and billows were left here and there on the ice. We hadn't traveled far when we were confronted with still rougher ice, and the cold November wind, head-on in our faces, tossed us about; the gusts seemed to increase in strength, and at moments we could scarcely keep our feet.

We kept plodding away under difficulties until we came to the bend of the river. Here, at this junction, we agreed that the wisest plan would be to leave the main channel for a short detour, thereby saving time and miles; then, too, the wild winds wouldn't lash our faces as they did on the open ice, for it seemed to be growing windier and windier, and colder and colder; besides, this shortcut would lead us through the low-lying tundra and lagoons, which were sheltered by the beautiful snow-covered spruce trees.

Greatly to our alarm, we hadn't gone many miles when the ice failed us as we were speeding over this virgin strip of waterway. Badly frightened, we hurried to the riverbank as quickly as possible, fairly holding our breaths, for the ice was visibly cracking portentously everywhere. It was apparent that it was most dangerous to proceed.

Well, what should we do now after this sudden surprise? It was far too late to retrace our steps, and it was perilous and foolhardy to continue; yet, on the other hand, some decision must be made quickly, for we couldn't afford the luxury of delay. Indeed, winter dusk would soon fold in around us and the cruel cold, being no respecter of persons, would freeze us without mercy.

While we were trying to think of some way out of this critical situation, we fed the dogs each a frozen fish, which they devoured in one gulp; then they lay down on their stomachs to rest. We ate our sandwiches and drank hot coffee for renewed energy, but in contrast to the dogs' quiet rest, we hopped around to keep warm.

It was a brilliant, clear day with a blinding whiteness covering the land, so much so that the glare of the sun hurt our eyes. In spite of the sunshine, the weather was distressingly cold, even in this secluded spot where the wind had almost ceased to blow. We were worried. We couldn't go back on the river, we didn't know the route across land, and we couldn't expect to see anyone in such an out-of-the-way place.

But luck was with us, for just at that moment a native going to the tundra to attend his traps came upon us most suddenly with his team of dogs. Our dogs, which had been so tired and woebegone, were now keen and alert, for they pricked up their ears and their graceful, bushy tails, almost leaping out of their harness in a mad dash for a fight. My husband grabbed the leader and saved the day—at least for the dogs. Just shortly before, we had petted our faithful and affectionate animals for their tireless efforts; now they were anything but peaceful and had turned into fighters.

This Eskimo was truly a blessing in a moment of despair; he pointed out a route through the forest that would eventually join the main river trail. We immediately moved according to his sign directions, but this trackless detour through the tall trees was a comical experience, and my sides ached from laughter as we attempted to untangle the dogs; we were both in hysterics. Since the stand of timber was close together, it was necessary to move slowly; as a result of our slow movement, one dog would wind himself around a tree, and before we could get him lined up, the others would be twisted around another tree, and thus it went—how many trees we missed and how many we hit were never counted, but after much ado we reached the snow plains of the river in safety. We were indeed thankful.

Though we were warmly clothed, we took turns riding on the handlebars to keep warm. My costume was the same bunglesome rigging that had kept me snug on the ride to the reindeer camp, but it wasn't flattering to my ego; however, on this trip I carried an overnight bag with feminine clothes to wear at the end of the day.

We traveled onward in the starlight, and soon we were shrouded in darkness, with spirits that were high, but with hands and feet that were decidedly cold. The dogs were beginning to lag, seemingly at the point of exhaustion, but we kept moving, for move we must.

Finally, our hearts leapt with joy and gratitude when we saw lights in the distance from a cluster of houses in the village to which we were going—as usual, all the dogs in the village announced our approach.

We were a sorry-looking bride and groom after being battered by the cold and wind and worried over the perils of the trail all day, but our souls were warm and happy. It was heaven to enter our friends' home, full of coziness, comfort, and hospitality. The very blood in our veins seemed to be frozen into ice.

Dinner was waiting and we were violently hungry. We had put our feet under many tables where the food was delicious, but none that we could recall surpassed this—our honeymoon—dinner. We had a roof over our heads instead of the bitter cold and the barren trail. It was a time for thanksgiving.

CHAPTER 19

Cabin on the Kuskokwim

Our new home was a cabin, for our new living quarters were still under construction. This frame hospital building, our home-to-be, was to have been completed long ago, but there were unforeseen obstacles to surmount before the contractor could present the finished product. In the first place, it was necessary to import skilled workmen from the States, and all building materials were shipped into the country, but the greatest handicap of all was the weather. Summer began when the ice cleared out of the river, which usually took place the last of May; frost was again in the air in the latter part of August. This short season warranted little time for progress—patience was a real virtue when men were laboring under these adverse conditions.

The delay created no hardship or discontent as far as we were concerned. This cabin was the coziest and happiest home that was ever mine to possess. It was a lodge where friendships bloomed, and the air was filled with peace and contentment— golden memories that even today are sweet but sorrowful.

This rustic cabin of one large room had been erected not far from the banks of the Kuskokwim River by an Eskimo youth whose mother had recently died and whose father, who was ailing, had lived only a few days longer. Since he was alone in the world, he rented his home to us, going to the reindeer camps as a herder.

This ambitious lad had transported the logs, one by one, from the nearby forest with his two husky dogs. These straight, telephone-pole-like logs were chiseled to fit the corners, flattened on two sides, and, by the help of his friendly neighbors, hoisted into place. The bark was left on the exterior, but the interior was peeled, sanded, and lastly shellacked and waxed. The cracks were filled with reindeer moss found on the tundra to keep the home warm and comfortable in the winter.

Our cabin home, nestled in a setting of pine trees, was comfortable, lacking in nothing essential, yet there was no modern equipment of any sort. Our supply of furnishings was meager: a bed, chest of drawers, homemade shelves for the library, bearskin rugs, writing desk, table, and four chairs, one of which was a rocker—these about cover everything. The tieback curtains of cheesecloth had an edge of open lace crocheted of carpet warp. A primus stove was used for light cooking, though our most substantial meals were eaten in the kitchen of the teacher's house, where Alice was still the cook— Lily slept over there for lack of space.

Our supply of water for all household purposes was hauled from the river by a native with his sled and dogs. In the winter a hole was cut through the ice, the water dipped out with buckets and then emptied into barrels for delivery. Most of the kitchens were supplied with three thirty-gallon barrels for storage. This difficult means of conveyance made us water-conscious, and none was ever wasted.

The lighting system was either compressed gasoline or kerosene, which afforded a brilliant light needed during the long winter nights. These utilities required time and foresight if they were to function satisfactorily; the lamps were pumped to a certain pressure each day, and the mantles must be kept in stock, since one touch rendered them useless after they were once burned to an ash.

The heating stove was a thirty-gallon gasoline tank propped on four legs off the floor. These legs were made by a tinner from a piece of steel. A hole had been cut for a ready-made door and an opening for the pipes. If the pipes were not installed in a certain way, the creosote formed by the heat and extreme cold ran down onto the floor and was not only messy but smelly. This stove was an unsightly commodity, rudely constructed, but it held four-foot logs, and one forgets false pride when comfort is more essential than beauty.

We had no daily paper, but the mail carrier delivered a monthly bulletin, featuring local news and outside headlines, printed by the wireless man at Holy Cross. Each person who wished to subscribe to these newscasts paid the sum of five dollars.

The government paid for our fuel, lights, water, and rent, so we were never disturbed over monthly bills for the utilities; the trader sent a statement for groceries. Telephones were not then installed in that district. There was little to buy, so we were not concerned over the high cost of living or whether we could balance the budget.

The windows of the cabin framed the contour of the rugged mountains to the east, and they also revealed the different scenes that were in action on the river. On the cold days we couldn't see through them; then the glass was converted into enchanting translucent pictures of fantastic hoary scenes, portrayed in a dainty frostwork of all descriptions. Anything that one could imagine was pictured by nature; cathedrals, animals, flowers, and trees were all magically represented.

The changing weather presented different views with the various temperatures; some days were gray with gentle rains covering the earth, but the summer supplied sunshine and fleecy white floating clouds, with a temperature that reached ninety degrees. Thunder was rarely heard even in the hottest weather. In comparison, the winter was cold, with the thermometer sometimes dropping to sixty below; in this severe weather the scenes out-of-doors were ineffably beautiful, depicting all the colors of the rainbow. The colder the days, the more fantastic were the colors in the heavens, especially in the evenings when the sun was going down. Then, on these frigid nights, the magnificent display of the northern lights left the observer completely lost in wonder and amazement. The awe-inspiring exhibitions of the Creator are beyond reproduction, for only God in his sanctuary can portray such an array of splendor.

The most intriguing sights from our cottage windows were of the Eskimo men, who escorted their families from place to place in tiny kayaks. The man and his wife sat back-to-back in the middle circle while he gracefully and skillfully piloted the tiny, light craft to safety. When he had anchored and gone ashore, the children then scrambled out of the covered space from either end into the open. How they could endure the roughness of the water and not be seasick was a mystery to me. They were duty bound not to rock the kayak, which was a light frame covered with birch bark, or it would easily turn over; yet I never heard of an accident.

The Eskimo trappers, who spent part of the winter in the hills, made a framework for their boats, then covered it with bearskins, fur inside and watertight, to transport their families back to the village for the fishing season. Their winter catch of furs, together with the dogs and sled which conveyed them to the mountains, were all loaded into this rudely constructed craft. The men probably wouldn't have passed the clearing out of any city, since they were loaded to the brim, but these men-of-the-woods travel on treacherous streams in light vessels without tragedy.

We could see the traders, who owned and operated a cabin-covered launch, going up and down the river either for business or pleasure. An occasional luxurious fishing yacht entered the channel in the interest of the Bureau of Fisheries. The river steamers plied up and down the way during the season, delivering the mail, freight, and passengers to all stations from Bethel to the Mount McKinley region; at the same time, they carried the outgoing mail, passengers, and freight of all commodities produced in the country, including furs, minerals, and fish by the loads. Bethel was the terminal for oceangoing liners, but a few of the freighters that didn't draw too much water came to our village of Akiak.

And of course, in the winter from these same windows dogs drawing sleds could be seen as they hurried back and forth across the river and over the trails. One good-for-nothing fellow who never planned for tomorrow daily hitched his one dog to the sled to go after wood before he could boil water for his morning tea.

Long caravans of reindeer and sleds came and went from the village, delivering supplies to the Lapp reindeer camps and to the government apprentices. Many of these sleds were equipped with flat, boatlike bottoms to keep the open streams in the late spring from wetting their wares. It was surely a captivating scene as we watched and listened to the sleds grinding in the snow. These sleds, drawn by reindeer, were bedecked with bells that jingled in the frosty air.

From our door, trails led out to the tundra—winter trails that men followed to trap, hunt, fish, and deliver wood. Travelers departed over the same way, some going to local communities, others to remote sections of the country, and a few on the first part of the long journey to the outside world.

Skiers met on the nearby hills, their favorite playground, where the snow by the constant thawing and freezing was packed like a boulevard, providing an easy passage for their sport. It was a humble ski resort with no comforts of a lodge and no ski tow to relieve the long and tiresome pull up the hill, but the woods echoed on the frosty air with much merrymaking and laughter.

Skaters gathered on the smooth, frozen lakes where they were sheltered from the wind, since the ice on the main river seldom froze smoothly enough for easy skating and the brusque, cold wind spoiled the fun.

We went the selfsame way, hand in hand, to ski, to skate, and to set our traps for a catch of furs. Time after time we visited these hidden snares, but without success. Consequently, the fur coat that was to have been mine never materialized. We evidently lacked the art and experience for successful trapping. Finally, when we went on our last trapping expedition, the traps had disappeared in the early spring thaw, and they couldn't be found.

CHAPTER 20

Our Son Is Born

When the hospital was completed, we moved to our new quarters on the first floor of that building. This home in contrast was much nicer, since the entire building was beautifully furnished by the government. But for all that, the log cabin with its pleasing plainness had been a comfortable place to live. More than that, it had possessed something that not even a castle could offer. A happy chapter of our lives was ended.

My position as teacher remained status quo, since married women were not barred from the schoolroom in Alaska; indeed, that part of the country was then so isolated that a man and his wife were more in demand than a single girl; then, too, it was late in the season to resign.

To administer first aid had been one of the responsibilities of my job, but my nursing capabilities were decidedly a minus quantity, and I had never got used to the sight of blood. I could shake down a thermometer, measure a dose of castor oil, massage with liniment and balsam, and do a few other things, like applying bandages or bathing sore eyes, but the task usually left me wilted, for I was scared to death that something awful might happen.

Now that the new hospital was in operation, this extra work wasn't on my calendar, but as much as I had worried

The riverboat *Quickstep*, docked at the Felder-Galen store,
Akiak. (Photograph by John Felder.
Courtesy of the Yugtarvik Regional Museum, Bethel, Alaska.)

The hospital at Akiak, built 1916–1918.
(From the collection of Dorothy Zimmerman.)

over the sick, I missed the Eskimo ladies, who had come to me for help when the nurse was out of the village. For instance, the wife of the village chief, a dear, wrinkled old lady who was ten times a great-grandmother, suffered intensely with a pain in her back. When school closed she was usually sitting at our house with her back to the heat, waiting to have the liniment rubbed into her aches. She expressed thankfulness in smiles for the treatment that eased her pain.

Her husband was a rare character and just a bit of a flirt, even though he was old and sometimes dirty. He went to visit his traps one Sunday evening, and to his surprise, he had captured a red-crossed fox. In the struggle to release his prize his leg was badly bruised, and it swelled up from the injury. On his return to the village he came immediately to the dispensary for care. While I was filling a bottle of chloroform liniment for him to take home for the application, he was busy rolling up his dirty pant leg. He chattered away in his language, trying his utmost to explain that he expected the same treatment accorded his wife. At last an interpreter succeeded in making him understand that I was not going to massage his leg. His wife, with her rheumatic arms, was handicapped, but his injury could easily be self-treated. Finally, he went on his way with feelings that were badly hurt.

Perhaps I should have favored the chief by rubbing down his leg, as he was a loyal friend. When the ice and snow covered our porches, he was always faithful with his snow shovel to keep them clean. More than that, when his daughter, Alice, was absent, he felt it his duty to help in every way possible, and liked to sit in our living room to tend the fires while I crossed the river to visit the girls or to shop at the store.

Fortunately, all that was necessary to win back his friendship was to invite him to a Sunday dinner after he had delivered a lengthy discourse in the Moravian church, where he often acted as a minister. He had been honored by our predecessors, so we felt that we should favor him as well.

My work was entirely apart from the hospital, but my husband did teach me how to make a hospital bed, and on one occasion I attempted to put a room in order. A friend of ours was entering the hospital for a major operation, and since we had been guests in her home, I hoped that this chamber would look extra attractive. It was Saturday, my holiday. I washed the windows, hung fresh, crisp curtains, changed the spread, waxed the floors, and even went so far as to spare one of our lovely rugs from the apartment. The room looked perfect to me, but when my husband came home that evening, he didn't see what I did; neither did he praise me for my labor of love. In his kind way he said, "You are a dear wife and teacher, yet it is evident that you are not a nurse." Well . . . what was left undone? Nothing that I could see. Then he added, "The very first thing a nurse does is to wash the grimy fingerprints from the white bed." How could I have been so blind? Later, when I came home, the rug was back in place—so that ended my career as a nurse.

When we discovered that a baby was on the way, we decided, inasmuch as I was teaching, to keep the secret to ourselves and not tell a soul.

That fall, while my husband was on an inspection trip to McGrath, he had purchased six yards of fifty-four-inch gorgeous dark blue serge. This material was bought with the idea of dresses for me for the schoolroom, but now the yardage would be made into maternity gowns and fashioned in such a way that no one would take notice as the time advanced. The skirts were cut and made into six gores with an elastic band inserted in the waistline to extend for the gradual increase. The waists were middies, trimmed in red soutache; then, to give the outfit a dressed-up look, a bright red tie was added; moreover, the dark material had a tendency to make one look smaller, so that too helped in the concealment.

One morning as I was on my way to school, a mother stopped to talk to me. She said, "I don't care if me Willie isn't pretty, but I want him smart." Then as the conversation continued, she informed me in a serious tone, "By and by, you plenty big." I answered in sort of an innocent way, "What!" Then she persisted, in spite of my opposition, "Yes, plenty big. I see it in your eyes." That was in the first stages, but one can't fool a native lady on that score.

The superintendent came from St. Michael in midwinter to pay his regular visit to our section of his enormous district. On this special trip, he was in a hurry to get back home. They were expecting the first baby, and since he was traveling with reindeer, there was little wonder that he was concerned. It happened that our house was filled with new employees, with no place for guests to sleep. The easiest solution was for me to spend the night with one of the girls while he shared my husband's bed.

That night, as these two men slept together, the superintendent expressed his pride over being an expectant father. He was a real man—soon to be a family man. My husband let him rave until, humanlike, it was more than he could stand; then he weakened and said, "Well . . . we, too, are expecting a baby." The next morning the superintendent dashed over to the schoolroom to offer his congratulations, so our secret was short-lived and definitely out.

My husband's specialty was obstetrics, and naturally his library was filled with volumes on the subject. I thought I would have a chance to read about the various changes of mothers, but before I had one spare moment to look at the books, he told me most emphatically not to take them from the shelves; he would take care of me and tell me anything that was necessary for me to know. From experience I learned that there is nothing so degrading as to be caught red-handed, especially by someone you love. I weakened when I thought that he was safely away on a trip. I slipped into the library for a special book that showed the horrible pictures of babies in a variety of shapes and deformities. I had just started reading when he came back unexpectedly. I hurriedly chucked the book on the shelf in the closet—a narrow escape. I would put it back as soon as the coast was clear, and read no more. But—by bad luck as usual—he went into the closet and there it lay before his very eyes.

In that country in those days, the big question was "What shall we do when the baby arrives?" Those who had the means traveled to Fairbanks, Seward, or Anchorage, and a few continued to the States, but such an expedition was very expensive.

Dr. Venters from Seattle, Washington, was, to our good fortune, in that country on an extended hunting trip; in fact, he had been a guest in our home between excursions here and there. Out of professional courtesy, he had offered his services, if we so wished, when the time was at hand. But the unexpected happened. When the baby sent out its SOS a day ahead of schedule, the doctor had not returned from up the river. Since there is no temporizing on such occasion, my husband had no alternative but to take over.

It was exciting while it lasted. Two hospital beds were exchanged for our bed. Lily, who slept upstairs, must have been disturbed in her sleep, for she rushed downstairs early to report that two hospital beds had been stolen during the night.

The tank of hot water in the sterilizing room could be heard as it upset on the floor; then, as I listened, the floor was being mopped. It was something new for my husband to be nervous, for he usually came downstairs whistling, no matter what medical procedures he had just done. When he carried the trays of water to our room, one of those turned over on the floor—no one suffered more than he when our baby boy arrived.

When the excitement was ended, I wanted to look after the nursing, but my husband insisted that he be called. About the third night, he was dead to the world from exhaustion and lack of help. He was called and called. Finally in his dreams he said, "Do it yourself."

He was in a jovial mood as he came in to look at his baby one morning, and as we admired him together, I remarked, "He isn't pretty, but like the Eskimo lady, I hope that he will be smart." My husband quickly answered, "He should be smart; he has been in school six months."

The coming of this baby into our lives seemed to make our world complete. Our home echoed with love, laughter, and dreams of things to be. We never pictured life without each other. It is truly wonderful that God in his divine plan releases only one day at a time, that there is no way to discover that one day those happy dreams must change. I went on cheerfully and contentedly but was to meet my sorrow just around the corner.

CHAPTER 21

My Husband's Death

The switch that suddenly turned on the lights of love, happiness, and laugher in my life just as unexpectedly cut them off. "One was taken and the other left." I was bewildered, bowed down with grief and despair.

One cold January morning a messenger with a grave face came to our door, and following him was a nurse from Bethel, a dear friend of ours. Her eyes were red and her face was lined with worry—their very looks told the sad story without words.

He was the bearer of a wireless message which read: "Dr. Lamb passed away at Old Hamilton, Alaska, December the twenty-third, nineteen hundred and eighteen. What is your wish as to burial?"

That fall my husband had been called into the army, but headquarters granted him a reprieve until after the birth of our baby boy. Soon after this happy event had taken place, he crossed to the Yukon on his way to Ruby, Alaska, traveling through ice and snow, to answer the call of the colors. When he arrived on the Yukon, the fighting was over and World War I had ended, but the dreaded disease of influenza was taking its toll of whites and natives alike on the lower Yukon.

The army did not now require his services, but he wasn't to

come home, for at once Governor Riggs of Alaska dispatched him to Nome, where at that time the malady seemed to be at its worst.

Boards of health were organized and stiff quarantines put into effect in order that the raging epidemic might be checked; the schools were closed and all social events were canceled. Tents were erected outside of the villages and towns so that travelers would have a place to sleep; they were afforded a tent stove with fuel for their comfort, since no traveler was permitted to enter a town of any size.

This was a most anxious time for all concerned, since at that time there were no radios and all the mail had been held up for future delivery.

My husband went down the Yukon ministering to the sick and carrying out the dead in the lonely, windswept villages in the most severe winter weather. On arriving in St. Michael he found many of the soldiers ill at the fort. After conferring with the doctor in charge at this place, he decided that instead of going on to Nome, it would be wiser to retrace his steps to the vicinity of Old Hamilton to direct the work in that section. He had no sooner reached this region when he was stricken with influenza or pneumonia while on the trail; his driver managed to reach the village, where our loved one soon passed away.

His body was then taken over the trail to St. Michael and placed in a metal casket to await our disposal. It was hard to realize that he would never be coming home.

When the news had circulated in the community that he was gone, many kind friends at once came to our house to extend their sympathy and to offer whatever assistance was needed in material things. Nowhere on earth could people have been more kind or sympathetic in times of distress; their kindness and helpfulness were without limit.

One Eskimo mother quietly slipped into my room, where I had gone to be alone with the baby. My face was buried deep in the baby's downy robe—he was only four months old. She clasped my hand and the baby's as she knelt in prayer. Her prayer was in her native tongue, not understandable to me, but God knew what she said.

We truly needed spiritual as well as material aid in that dark hour. When one is taken who is dearer than life itself, it really takes faith to believe "that life is ever lord of death, and love can never lose its own."

Letters of sympathy came from far and near and from people in all walks in life. One arrived from Mother Superior, but she didn't realize when she wrote me that she had met me on the *Victoria*. It was written as follows:

> Fort St. Michael, Alaska
> January 15, 1919.

Dear Mrs. Lamb,

> Your husband passed through here on his way to his mission of heroic doctrine, and all St. Michael sang his praises.
>
> Deep in the depths of every noble heart echoed the cheer to the magnificent young man, whose face was turned steadfastly toward duty.
>
> But the anthem had not died on the frosty air, when the wail for his death came mingling with it.
>
> Dear Mrs. Lamb, that is why I, a stranger, venture to intrude upon your grief in the great human fellowship of sympathy and sorrow. . . . Judith brings its promise in my heart, "In Thy Providence hast thou placed Thy Judgments."

> Sincere sympathy,
> Sr. M. Amadieus,
> Supt. of the Ursulines of Alaska.

The book of Judith wasn't to be found in my Protestant Bible, but one of the fathers from the Catholic mission of Holy Cross, Alaska, who made our home his overnight stop when en route to the missions in our district presented me with a version of the Catholic Bible.

The affairs which we fret and worry over seldom take place, but the happenings that mean the most in our lives are decided once and for all without our knowledge and before we have time for anxiety.

My future course had seemed to be a lifetime of happiness; never for one instant did I entertain the idea that any tragedy could end my enchanted dream; but death walked boldly into our midst the twenty-third of December. The messenger arrived with a radiogram the tenth of January, and early in February the mail carried a letter which he had written of his last days of living. My brother Ben, who was in the army in France, read the tragic news before it reached our remote section of the world.

My cross at the time seemed hard to bear. We were confronted with a grim struggle to face the readjustments of life; it took courage and determination to take up the burden and face the future, but we don't fold up in a crisis, for there are resources we never knew we had. My precious baby was my ray of light in a suddenly darkened world.

My husband's mother, who shared our home that winter, was a great source of inspiration. Now she looked white and shocked, but she was surprisingly brave. The past year her daughter Helen had died, and only the last week she had asked to have the letters destroyed, saying tremulously, "I can't bear to burn them, but there is no reason to keep them longer." An ominous feeling had crept over me.

Mother was in her sixties, but her brown eyes were still young; her hair was graying, and her hands were wrinkled and blue-veined. She was rather plump and often said, "I shouldn't have allowed myself to grow stout." She belonged to the old order of aristocracy. She couldn't forget that hers was one of the first families of Detroit, and even in Alaska she left her calling cards. Mother was the grand old matriarch while her son was living, but now she grew mellow and tender with understanding. Thoughtfully she commented, "I have seen most of life, but I am sorry for you and the baby; you have lost all that a husband and father mean to a home—love, companionship, and protection; a mother and a baby are only part of a home." Little did she dream that she would be living with me, her daughter-in-law, for thirteen years to come.

The messenger had traveled to Bethel to bring back Mrs. Joaquin, a nurse, with him. He feared that the news of Dr. Lamb's death might be more than his mother could bear. It was a long, out-of-the-way trip, with the cold wind howling up the river, but they arrived in Akiak at four o'clock in the morning.

Mrs. Joaquin remained with us for a week, leaving her home and six-month-old baby in the care of friends, but that is the way people do in Alaska. She was a large, bighearted, jovial Dutch girl, fresh from a trip to Holland. We needed someone big and strong and gay to keep us from sinking—she was our lifeline.

We were like wounded animals. In every turn we suffered. Our spirits were shattered in the wreckage of a happy life, but no matter how hard the blow, it was up to us to adapt ourselves to new changes and new problems of the future.

We would return to the States, but exactly when and how was the question until the government wired us to go over the trail to the Yukon to await the opening of spring navigation. A comfortable steamer for passengers might not arrive on our river that spring. Aircraft were not flitting in and out as today.

CHAPTER 22

Return to Seattle

The life that had been so full of happiness now passed with little meaning; but at last three months had slipped away, and the fragrance of spring was in the air. The birds were returning, and even the pussy willows were in bloom. It was time for us to leave for the outside world.

An Icelander, Mr. Goodmansen, with a team of seven beautiful dogs, one or two having been on the winning team in the Nome races, was engaged to transport us over the highway to the Yukon. This man was a past master in handling a dog team, as he had just returned from an extensive fur-buying trip that took him into the very heart of Russia. For some unknown reason that country had detained him at the pleasure of her rulers, but Uncle Sam was his protection; even so, it was some time before he chould shake the mud from his boots to be free to travel home. Mr. Goodmansen, a friend of my husband's, had offered to make the trip to the Yukon. When he came to make travel plans, he picked up my baby boy. It was then that his blue eyes grew wet with tears. His heart was touched; he wasn't thinking only of my fatherless babe, but he, too, was the father of an infant son, born while he was in Russia, whom he hadn't seen.

Before he would be at liberty to give us a helping hand, he

was obliged to make a short business trip up the river. This delay would be of little consequence, since a long wait was in the offing for us at the end of the journey. He left at once, assuring us that he would return promptly and adding, "Don't worry, we will take care of you."

While he was away we went about the perplexing business of packing, without much enthusiasm, but it had to be done. Many problems and complications confronted us. What to take and what to leave behind? One doesn't realize how fast articles accumulate until it is time for a move.

Our dearest possession to be left behind was our Lily, but Mr. and Mrs. Kilbuck gladly gave her a home. They changed her name at once to Mary instead of Lily, since the naughty children too often called her a black Lily and this constant teasing kept her spirits dampened.

In the course of the next years, Mr. Kilbuck suddenly died, and for that reason Mrs. Kilbuck then packed her possessions. She, too, came south to make her home, and Mary accompanied her.

Mary loved and enjoyed life in the West, although she was far removed from her native land; she added joy to the broken home of which she was a part; still, this new way of life wasn't lasting, for she fell victim to tuberculosis as she entered her teens, passing away after months of illness.

We temporarily engaged a little fat mixed-blood girl named Sally from up the river to help with the baby and do what she could. She was painfully inefficient compared with Alice; still she was valuable as a nurse girl, taking the baby out for airings and thus giving us more time to prepare for the move. She liked to eat and often said, "Bear fat better than butter." The peanut butter went like magic, leaving the marks of her fingers in the jar.

We were crowded for space but Sally refused to sleep in Mary's room. The room had been intended for a bathroom, but for some reason the fixtures didn't arrive on the fall boat, so it had served other uses. First it was a storeroom. Then it had been a death cell until a larger room replaced it; when a ward patient was doomed to die, he was removed from the sick and placed alone for his last hours. Mary had been thrilled to have the room for herself when it was no longer needed for the hospital. With Sally it was different; "I won't sleep in that room, I might die," she cried.

Alice was now separated from her third husband, so she came over to offer her assistance. She had often left us in the lurch, but she was a godsend in our time of need. Now she seemed full of compassion—it was the only time she was ever seen to part with a tear, except in a rage.

Our packing was nearing completion. Mother and I had no concern about our clothing except to keep warm. The baby was the problem in planning for his comfort for three days; by leaving Akiak early one afternoon we should arrive in Marshall before dark on the third day. Three changes of the baby's oldest wearing apparel were laid aside for the trail. Rubber pants were not available. Soiled and wet baggage is annoying in any land, especially when frozen; each day we would throw away these old garments and forget them.

Now we were ready to go, but no driver. Two weeks had passed. What was keeping him? There could be many reasons for delay. Transportation with a dog team or boat in that country was seldom on schedule. Engine trouble happened unexpectedly in the summertime, and a sick dog in winter spoiled the plans. Perhaps the driver was ill or the dogs' feet too sore to keep up the pace day after day. Whatever the cause, he was still absent.

April brought a sudden rise in temperature and warm sunshine, causing much concern over the condition of the trail; the snow was melting like a candle before our eyes. Soon there would be no sledding.

My patience with the strain of uncertainty was fast becoming exhausted, and the hopelessness of it all was exasperating.

Decisions were often made quickly and without too much deliberation, but right or wrong, some action had to be taken if we were to go to the Yukon that spring.

We waited for a while for Mr. Goodmansen to return; then with much difficulty we engaged another driver with a second-rate team. This sourdough was a tall Canadian with curly, tousled red hair, who seldom wore a hat. When he wasn't wearing mukluks, his soiled wool breeches were tucked into wraparound gaiters. A red plaid mackinaw was his favorite coat. This man was heartless and preoccupied with his own interests and comforts, but he had traveled widely in Alaska and knew the trails. He wasn't made of the same stuff as most Alaskans.

Not every man would care to shoulder the responsibility for a grandmother, a mother, and a wee baby, so we couldn't afford to be too choosey, especially since most of the men who had a destination to make had left town before the spring thaw.

Now we were all set to go, which was a relief, but delay seemed endless. This second man asked for three days' grace in which to get married—a most sane and worthy reason for a bachelor, but who would have him?

The day before our scheduled departure both men arrived in the hamlet. Mr. Goodmansen had been delayed because of illness, saying, "I am indeed sorry to have kept you waiting." The other man again was quite different. He immediately advanced his price, adding, "It is much more expensive for two to live than one." The Icelander was asking for nothing, save a chance to help in time of need. The two men were as different as night and day.

We were glad to have engaged two drivers, for Mother needed a sled all to herself for back support; besides, it would have been a ticklish situation to have discharged the second man after all the difficulty in the hiring. Another man, Big Hans by nickname, big in size, big in every way that stood for generosity and unselfishness, was going on a freighting trip to the Yukon, so he took our overflow baggage in his empty sled, making three in the caravan.

My trunk had been packed to go for three months. It proved to be a jinx every time it was used. To have chopped it up for kindling wood would have been a pleasure in more ways than one. It was silly to have packed it in the beginning. Every time an article was needed, it was sure to be at the bottom. Now— this baggage was roped and ready. Thank goodness! But all the trouble didn't end here. When the men came to lash the trunk, it was considerably larger than the sled. It was necessary to leave it behind. To take the place of the trunk, the men calmly and quickly nailed a box together, and my possessions were dumped into it with no semblance of order.

An Eskimo youth named Peter Wassili, who was going to the States on his first trip, took a fancy to the chest, so I quickly and gladly sold it to him. I hope never to lay eyes on it again. It was the same luggage that was on the wrecked steamer, causing so much trouble in the first place.

The last iron in the fire had been pulled, the dirt had been swept in the corner with a broom placed over it for good luck to the newcomers, and we had looked in every room to see that nothing was forgotten. Now we were ready to leave.

Many kind friends from both sides of the river were present to bid us good-bye. Alice slipped five dollars into my hand, whispering, "Money me give you to hire baben's washing done on the way out." The tenderness in this kind act started the tears flowing. Even though Mary was in better hands, she was alongside pulling on my heartstrings, making it hard to part with her. Indeed, these were choking moments; both the natives and whites had shared alike in our happiest and saddest days. Some were the praying kind, others the doing, and some were both, but they were all dear to us, so the parting brought more sadness.

The trail was somewhat soft that evening, causing the sled

to slip and slide, but there was no concern as to its falling apart; neither was I apprehensive about the sleigh tipping over, but that very thing suddenly happened on a sloping hillside. The accident was anticipated in time to hurl the baby over into a snowdrift to avoid mashing him against the sides of the sled; consequently no one was hurt save for a scratch on the child's face, but the wee tot was badly frightened, since the spill happened so suddenly. As an aftermath, he cried and cried and eventually sobbed himself to sleep.

This was the third bump in one week. The first time he had wiggled from the center of the bed, and later was found on the floor with no ill effects. The second mishap was a tumble on the ice. We had gone a short distance up the river with a homemade sled, a milk box attached to runners, to purchase fresh eggs at the price of a dollar fifty a dozen. Going down the incline on the return to the river, it seemed impossible to handle both the sled and the eggs. Thoughtlessly I protected the eggs, but left the sled free to slide on its own accord, thinking it would land safely on the river, but to my shame, the baby tumbled headlong onto the ice, cutting his tender, rosy cheeks. Thus, early in life he learned to take the bumps.

The task of holding a child above the rim of the sled to avoid being crushed proved most paralyzing to my arms. Anticipating this discomfort, we started on our way with a number of pillows for arm support, but they were very soon missing. We thought that they had been forgotten at the first night's stop, but to my disgust, they were found at the end of the journey, chucked into a gunnysack, making a more comfortable seat on the gee pole for the second driver.

We were covering a short distance of ten miles that first evening, but the length of driving seemed infinitely long. We kept looking for the village long before it was time to arrive, but trailways are like highways; as soon as the top of one hill is reached, another looms up in the distance. At last, out and beyond, we spied the village where we were to take refuge for the night.

A cabin of two rooms had been engaged earlier; consequently we knew what to expect in the class of our hotel. This nutshell of a cabin provided homemade bunks on which we placed our fur robes and blankets for bedding. The men slept on the floor, which couldn't have been too comfortable, but these travelers are not fussy when they are sheltered from the cold weather—frequently men have dug into a snowbank when they failed to reach their destination or were lost in a storm.

We went to bed before our regular time at home since we were to leave early the next morning for the long day's drive; then, too, we were drowsy and weary from the afternoon's jaunt. The sandman had closed the eyes of my chubby, tender little bundle, so he was tucked away for the night before we had eaten our dinner.

For some reason, neither Mother nor I could sleep. It may have been the coffee, and the springless beds were quite a contrast from the mattresses just left behind; yet, taking one thing with another, the feverish strain of the day, the leaving of what had meant so much—that was the real reason. We tried to concentrate on sleep, but our bodies were subservient to our minds. Not until we were completely exhausted did we forget the world and its cares.

The next morning we were haggard and worn when it was time to be about, and the bed felt more comfortable. Then we had the urge to sleep another hour, but the baby, true to type, was awake early in the morning; more than that, we could smell the aroma of coffee in the next room, which meant haste to be on the trail.

That morning we ate our breakfast on a little rustic table and sat on wooden benches. Usually the dishes were white or gray enamal, but to my surprise, these were china. They could have been Spode or Haviland, that I don't remember, but they were a notable contrast to the rest of the surroundings.

The breakfast was served by the owner of the little inn, and on the menu were sourdough hotcakes, bacon, eggs, and fruit. All this food at one meal would be considered a luxury with today's high cost of living, but that fare was to last us until the end of the day, save for a small lunch at noon.

The baby wasn't even considered, and we didn't tarry along the way for his regular meals; fortunately, he was a nursing child, who could be served a snack very conveniently as the dogs bounded onward.

Our few belongings, which had been placed inside the cabin to keep warm for the next day's travel, were once more re-loaded; again we were on the lone trail with a few lag-last stars shining in the cold, clear sky.

The snow had melted to some degree the previous day, but the night's freezing had left a crust; as a result, the traveling was easier and faster in the morning, and the time quickly slipped away. Before we realized what was happening, an igloo, snuggled in the hollow of a valley, loomed before our eyes. This place was the winter quarters of a trapper, a sort of halfway house, where men were always welcome to stop for food or spend the night.

It was a good feeling to rest for a short time, for our limbs had gone to sleep from being tucked in the covers so tightly for warmth, and furthermore, the baby had been wiggling and squirming no matter how hard I tried to keep him quiet. Wearing damp diapers from post to post was something new in his young life—thus early in childhood he learned "What can't be cured, must be endured."

As usual, the dogs flopped down on their stomachs, since they were weary from going at a lively clip all morning—dogs are usually served but one meal each day, but these were given a tidbit for encouragement.

We crawled down into the igloo for a sandwich and a cup of

tea, but loss of time was a major liability with miles and miles ahead of us to be covered before nightfall, so once again we were on the way.

The day, which was warm and sunny, caused the snow to melt, and for that reason, the trail was much heavier and slower, working a hardship on men and dogs alike. Our beautiful team, which had pulled and tugged so faithfully, was now a picture of despair as the dogs strained every muscle with heads and tails down.

We were not far from the stopping place for the night, but the going was treacherous. It happened that we reached the Yukon just at dusk, but on our arrival we found that the melting snow had caused the river to rise, leaving water on the edges of the main river to be forded. Under these circumstances, the men were obliged to measure every step across the river with a pole to avoid a catastrophe. It was one o'clock in the morning when we finished our day's travel. We were all at the point of exhaustion, especially the dogs.

No hotel could have been more inviting than this shelter, which was a trader's store, and our bed was the floor. The mattress was a wolf robe and the cover was a robe of muskrat skins. The baby, having slept all day, was now in a playful mood; consequently, when we awoke in the morning he had somehow scooted across the room and was found in the opposite corner of the store, cheerfully eating onion skins out of a box.

After nearly three days of harried travel we arrived in the little, bleak village of Marshall, not too much chafed by the outing that lacked the comforts of our routine home life. We surely owed our men escorts a debt of gratitude for a safe journey through which they had labored under unexpected difficulties.

The Board of Health in that section had reserved board and room for us at the village roadhouse during our six weeks' sojourn in that town. This inn was owned and operated by a dear middle-aged Swedish spinster, Miss Cleave, whose reputation for kindness to her guests was unexcelled; for that reason we were looking forward with pleasure to our stay with her.

When we arrived in Marshall that afternoon, Miss Cleave was at the door to meet us, though she had no idea when we would make our appearance. When I introduced myself as Mrs. Lamb, her face showed surprise and perhaps a touch of disappointment. Then she immediately smiled and laughingly said, "Well, you are most certainly not the same girl that I had pictured you to be."

How often have we framed mental pictures of someone whom we have never met, and invariably they turn out to be the very opposite of our expectations.

My husband, whom she had known in his traveling over the country, was a ruddy-faced, sturdy outdoor man, very fair, with light blue eyes. He stood five feet eleven, possessing a jovial disposition that immediately electrified the very atmosphere with joyfulness wherever he happened to be.

She was evidently disappointed in not finding me a "frail creature" or a "petite blond beauty." My looks were quite the opposite; my weight was one hundred twenty pounds; I stood a mere five feet four in my bare feet, and my mukluks added little to my stature. My hair was dark brown, bordering on black, I had deep brown eyes, and my features were decidedly Welsh. I really wasn't bad looking. Perhaps it was the mukluks that surprised her.

After the first shock, her welcome was most cordial. She immediately turned over the best part of the house to us: a huge front room that was otherwise used as a lounge for travelers. This rendezvous was equipped with both cooking and sleeping facilities, and every provision had been made for our comfort—a haven of rest it was indeed.

What a relief! The men unloaded our possessions—homemade trunk, warm bags, pillows, robes, and all the baby's paraphernalia—squarely on the middle of the floor. It was a chaos to be sure, but in our leisure time, when the kinks were out of our limbs and the blood circulating normally, the disordered world reverted to tidiness.

Miss Cleave invited us to share her meals until we could supply our cupboard. We were to be her guests for dinner that first evening, and the next morning she had baked her favorite Swedish coffee bread for breakfast. Thus it went, for her store of supplies was well stocked—and more. From that time on we cooked and ate together, sharing the work and expense as one complete family—a happy plan for all concerned.

The baby soon won his way into her affections; she enjoyed Mother Lamb, who was a well-read, interesting conversationalist; and if I didn't measure up to her expectations, she never again showed her disillusionment.

Miss Cleave was a middle-aged spinster, born in Sweden, but a naturalized American. She was a capable, pleasingly plain woman with smiling blue eyes. Sometimes her face seemed set in sadness, but she could quickly change her countenance to that of smiles when a guest arrived. Her heart and lodge typified the very essence of viking characteristics with an atmosphere of dignity—none finer in that section of the world. The mushing sourdoughs truly found her inn the "House by the Side of the Road."

She loved my little Frank tenderly and affectionately. She was never too busy at her work to take time out to cuddle and amuse him. One day, while he was waiting to be fed, she sat at the table with his chubby little hands around her neck. With much feeling she said, "You are a bundle from heaven, too good for this earth." A moment later, in a tantrum, he kicked over his milk. Surprised, she remarked, "I guess you will live."

Mother displayed calm grace of manner, courage, and common sense in this hour of trial, but we knew by her sad eyes that her heart was breaking from the loss of her only son. Often she kept to her bed because her health was failing,

failing not so much because she was aging and frail, but grief, the ruggedness of traveling, and the pain of tragedy sapped her strength.

She tried to be brave for the sake of me and the baby. She was most kind and considerate until I gave way in tears. Then she seemed hard-hearted and unsympathetic, but long since have I thanked her for her levelheadedness in times of despair. When I cried, she lost no time in telling me that this was my cross to bear, and that it was my duty to meet bravely whatever the future might hold in store for me. She had seen more living than I, and she probably saved me from being completely overwhelmed with self-pity.

Usually during the day my feelings were suppressed and buried in the day's activities. But at times, great surges of grief and loneliness came over me. At night the dam of pent-up tears burst forth and my pillow was wet with weeping—all of no avail, for nothing can bring back the yesterdays.

This town of Marshall was a mere village built on the banks of the Yukon and settled by hardworking miners. Two stores supplied the villagers and also the outlying districts with food and clothing; and the traders purchased furs from the natives. The territory provided a grade school for the white children, whose number was small, but the natives who could present a clean health record and measure up to certain standards were enrolled. The community also afforded a jerry-built show house, the roadhouse where we lived, and a dance hall. These, in fact, made up the town's social center.

Those in the town showered us with kindness. We were invited out to dinners beautifully served on linens and with dishes that any home in the States would be proud to display. My eyes widened in one home, that of Mr. and Mrs. George Marsh, where the chicken was cut for serving with a sterling silver scissors designed for that purpose.

Not only in the village were we entertained, but the miners' wives asked us to their homes, where we enjoyed their hospitality in the peace and quiet of their surroundings out by the gold fields where they dug for the rich metal.

Eskimo ladies were lavish in their gifts of baskets to us and moccasins and mittens for the baby. These presents were tokens of appreciation of past favors rendered by his father.

The tiny infant was in need of footgear, for the wee pair he had, now scuffed and worn, had been given to me by his father when he first came into the country, in truth, before I scarcely knew him. He had been out on a sick call, when a native lady presented him with a new pair of beautiful child's moccasins. When he returned to the government house where we all lived under one roof, he gave these boots to me, saying in a jovial mood, "Put these in your hope chest and we will use them one day." They were presented in gaiety and used in sadness.

The six weeks ended very abruptly; in fact, we were far from being ready, since we hadn't expected to be leaving for two or three days. To our complete surprise, about two o'clock in the morning the shrill whistle of a steamer aroused us from a deep sleep, and to be sure, it was the riverboat *Sarah,* following the wake of the ice; furthermore, it was the ship on which we were booked to sail for our connections with the liner *Victoria* in St. Michael.

It was now the first of June and daylight on the Yukon at that hour in the morning; so I bounded out of bed, dressed, and dashed to the dock to inquire how long the steamer would be in port. To my surprise and delight, Captain Lancaster was still the master of the *Sarah.* It was good to see a familiar face, for he was the same genial, thoughtful captain as when we girls came up the river. He told me that he would give us two hours to make the steamer—with that I was gone. A burden lifted, for I knew that he wouldn't sail without me.

What should be done first with everything helter-skelter? The laundry had not yet been delivered and my homemade trunk was out being repaired—nothing was packed.

Miss Cleave washed, fed, and dressed the baby, which was a

real pleasure to her, though the tears trickled down her cheeks in every move as he cooed and smiled at her efforts in that early morning. It was, indeed, a mad scramble, with our worldly goods thrown together, but we made the ship with a few minutes to spare.

This dear lady had made our stay most pleasant, taking out the clouds and replacing them with sunshine in ways that we never dreamed were possible. The next year she was ill with a cancer ailment, caused by a fall, and very soon she passed away. She was then buried in the Northland—the country that she dearly loved.

Our passage to the States could be likened to "All Gaul," for it was divided into three distinct parts: the trail, the river, and the ocean. The long, winding trail, which was the shortest, but the most strenuous, section of the entire journey, was now behind us, with the fretting and inconveniences soon forgotten.

We were now aboard the good ship *Sarah,* and at last we were bound for St. Michael on the second installment of our prolonged trip home and "me papa's house." After two hours of feverish haste, we could finally breathe a sigh of relief, rest, and relax, a calm after the storm.

We were the only two ladies traveling on the steamer this first trip of the season, so for that reason we had our choice of the two largest staterooms on the boat. These spacious accommodations were most acceptable, inasmuch as we needed a roomy place to organize our baggage with some semblance of tidiness. In the present mess it was necessary to ransack everything to find the needed articles.

We were no sooner out in midstream when the second familiar face came to my cabin door. This time it was the chief engineer, Mr. Hyde, a bighearted, fatherly man whom I had met when we first went up the Yukon. He immediately said, "I will fill the tubs in the engine room and then heat the water with steam if at any time you wish to do the baby's laundry."

May Wynne Lamb and her son, Frank, taken
while she was still teaching in Alaska in the 1920s.
(From the collection of Dorothy Zimmerman.)

Well . . . I didn't want to wash. The past two hours of lively confusion had left me breathless, with no backbone or frame of mind to work. This surprising offer was most kind and thoughtful of him, for soiled clothes are always accumulating, and still more with an infant to care for. I couldn't think of anything nice to say on the spur of the moment, but thanked him in a feeble sort of way. We would be in St. Michael in three days, and the child's togs should keep him fresh for that length of time.

Usually I like to wash, but it never was the uppermost pleasure in my domestic operations, even with the best of equipment. Now would be a good time to procrastinate, at least for the time being. Alice was more than ever appreciated for the way she kept the hamper free of soiled baby clothes, and more than that, they had not been so beautifully done since we left home seven weeks ago.

We sailed down the broad river with the huge, stern paddles implementing the drive of the current. This was the same highway that my husband had followed during the winter as a frozen trail, but in contrast, we reached Old Hamilton on a beautiful, warm summer day.

While the freight was being loaded, we went ashore to thank each one personally who had a share in my husband's last days of living. A memorable, sad Sunday.

The steerage section on this steamer was more than crowded with many nationalities of men who were being transported by way of the interior to fish for a new cannery, a place that was just being established on the mouth of the Yukon River near the Bering Sea. This new site, which was called Waddum's Bluff, was named after the superintendent of the company.

The steamer also carried part of the cannery equipment, so instead of going directly to St. Michael, as we had supposed, the boat made a detour through one of the other channels farther south to deliver the cargo of men and supplies to this new port. The steamship company had agreed to feed this multitude of workers until both the huge tents for kitchen and dining room were set up for service. This time was intended to cover a period of two days, but three had passed before they were ready for business.

This extra third day of feeding this army of men dug deep into the ship's supplies, which was no little concern to the chief steward on the *Sarah*. We had the boat's crew and the passengers to serve until he could replenish his store in St. Michael. These three days were intensely interesting as we watched the city of tents being erected to house and feed the many workers. The cannery had previously been installed for action, so it was ready to operate when the fish were delivered.

It was an interesting sight to watch the loaded boats of fish being transposed to canned salmon with cleanliness, efficiency, and ease. The finished product was turned off the assembly line and into cartons for delivery to the States in no time at all. This was a decided contrast from the miniature canning outfit that the nurse and I had used to can our winter supply of salmon.

There were only two white ladies in camp at that time; one boarded the boat at Pilot Station to join her husband, a cook, at the cannery; the other was a seasoned sourdough nurse who had set up her dispensary to administer first aid.

We left Waddum's Bluff late that evening, and it was shortly after midnight when we passed out of the Yukon flats into the cold blue waters of the Bering Sea. It was a glorious morning, with none of the usual June icebergs in sight; under these conditions we would soon be in St. Michael.

It so happened that a sick man, an officer on the ship, was causing great concern among his shipmates, and the captain's face registered uneasiness lest the ice in the Bering Sea delay his entry into St. Michael, where this patient could be hospitalized and under a doctor's care. For this reason alone, it was good to think that we were steaming into port with no obstacles to bar a speedy passage.

To our complete surprise, our movements were thwarted within an hour after clearing the river bar. Almost immediately we were embraced on all sides with huge, powerful cakes of sparkling crystal ice, shining like millions of diamonds, which not only barred our passage, but ground ominously against three freight barges safely tied around our ship.

We surely would have been crushed to the bottom of the sea but for these stout scows. One being securely fastened and pushed ahead of the steamer and one made fast to each side of the boat were a protection from the huge icebergs that would have gouged holes in our floating palace. For ten long days we drifted with the ice.

By this time the baby didn't have a clean change of clothing. Something had to be done about the emergency, so the cabin boy was hired to wash what was needed to tide us over. Much to my surprise, when they were delivered, the dresses were so full of starch that they cut his tender, chubby little neck, and the diapers irritated his sensitive skin. The cabin boy laughed, saying, "I washed them the same as a man's shirt."

The odds were evidently against me, so it was necessary, then and there, to resign myself to that task of washing. I went down to the engine room, and true to his offer, the engineer prepared the tubs and put up the line while the members of the crew took turns as nursemaids. Every night while the engines were not in action, tiny shirts, dresses, diapers, and the many things in a child's layette were dried, and some of mine were added.

From that time on, every day was a merrymaking laundry day—even Sunday. What I imagined would be drudgery magically turned into a real pleasure. We all had a jolly good time. When the men grew weary of the poker game, they placed the baby on the table, where he hurled the poker chips helter-skelter as fast as they could pick them up.

The kindness and courtesy of those bighearted men on the

Sarah, from the captain of the ship down to the busboys, who entertained the baby every day and each day at mealtime while I ate my food in peace, will always be an outstanding page in my book of memories.

We entered the port of St. Michael after nearly a fortnight of anxiety for those on land. They were greatly concerned over the whereabouts of our ship, since it was reported to be sinking in the ice jam. Under these conditions, it was little wonder that they were worried, but on the contrary, we were not the least frightened, for we had faith in our captain, who had weathered other serious blockades.

When we reached St. Michael we were obliged to wait for ten days on the sailing of the steamer *Victoria.* She, too, had encountered much ice on her way north, and naturally this caused the delay on the homeward-bound trip.

During this leisure time I went up to the Catholic home to call on Mother Superior, but it was an unexpected disappointment fo find her too ill to receive visitors. On this first sailing of the *Victoria,* she was being transferred to Seattle for medical treatment and more efficient care. A real bed had replaced one of the bunks for her comfort on the outgoing journey—thus, it was by chance that we came north together and, likewise, went south on the same ship, but under widely different circumstances.

The United States marshal had asked me to call at his office, where my husband's personal effects were in his care: his sleeping bag, his clothing, and his wristwatch. It had been nearly six months since he had died. Now I lived again those heartbreaking days. Old emotions and memories rushed over me. I wanted him more than all of life, but he was beyond my embrace. The watch was placed in my purse, but the other possessions were left behind. I left the office in tears.

As I wheeled the baby down the bumpy, wavering sidewalk a few Eskimos were on the sidelines. Suddenly they let out a terrible wail as they saw the baby, saying, "Him face all the same him papa's"—father and son couldn't have looked more alike.

My husband's body was being shipped in a metal casket by the same steamer on which we were taking passage. A solemn and bitter arrangement. Life for him was over at twenty-nine. It didn't seem fair. He had lived abundantly and well. Why, with the curtain of life's drama drawn, had he left the stage so soon?

We were afforded beautiful weather and smooth sailing on the way south. When we reached the port of Seattle, we entrained for Blissfield, Michigan, where our dear one was laid to rest in a grave beside his Uncle Hal on the ninth of July, 1919.

I was no longer the carefree girl who had gone to Alaska. I had had a world of experience, much of it happy, some of it heartbreaking. Life had dealt me a staggering blow, but it wasn't the end of everything. There was much of my beloved in the baby, and I was ready to face the future.

AFTERWORD

*

After traveling to Blissfield with her mother-in-law, Mrs. Wyman Lamb, for the burial of her husband, May visited her
family in Kansas, then went to Stamford, Connecticut, to stay
with members of her late husband's family. May decided in
December to return to Alaska and, with her son, Frank, and
Mrs. Lamb, left for Bethel in August. "On August 17, 1920,"
she wrote, "We went back to Bethel, reaching there five weeks
later. Came in via Skagway, Dawson, Russian Mission—
crossed portage—four days from Yukon to Kuskokwim."
May taught in Alaska for ten more years—two years in Bethel,
two years in Klukwan and Haines, one year in Flat, one year in
Hecata, three years in Juneau, and one year in Gustavus. She
spent some of her summers in Seattle and finally returned there
to live. Frank Lamb, Jr., graduated from the University of
Washington in Seattle and received a Ph.D. in physics from
Northwestern University in Evanston, Illinois. He served as a
captain in the army in World War II and as a scientist in various
laboratories after the war.

When I first met my Aunt May in Seattle in 1936, she was in
the construction business. She owned three houses and was
building another. As an eleven-year-old, I was impressed by
her dealings with workmen and found her kind but formida-

ble, for she was something of a legend in our family. After World War II, May made a trip around the world, touring Europe alone when in her sixties and then joining a tour for China and Japan. She settled in Palo Alto, California, where she lived until her death in 1973. Her son, Frank, died in 1981.

NOTES

Introduction

1. *Thirteenth Census of the United States Taken in the Year 1910*, vol. 3 (Washington, D.C.: Government Printing Office, 1913), pp. 1133, 1139.

2. Wendell H. Oswalt, *Alaskan Eskimos* (San Francisco: Chandler Publishing Co., 1967), p. 7.

3. Ibid., p. 3.

4. John Collier, *Alaska Eskimo Education* (New York: Holt, Rinehart and Winston, 1973), pp. 11–12.

5. Henry M. Michael, ed., *Lieutenant Zagoskin's Travels in Russian America, 1842–1844: The First Ethnographic and Geographic Investigation in the Yukon and Kuskokwim Valleys of Alaska* (Toronto: University of Toronto Press, 1967), p. 257.

6. There had been a law providing for schools in Alaska since 1884, when Congress had passed an act directing the secretary of the interior "to make needful and proper provision for the education of children of school age . . . without regard to race." The first schools had been operated in cooperation with the Christian missionaries who were already there and who had established a number of mission schools. This system was abandoned in the mid-1880s. At the time May went to Alaska, education was offered to approximately 60 percent of the native children, "as many as can be reached under present appropriations." In 1914 there were sixty-one native schools. See A. W. Greely, *Handbook of Alaska* (New York: Charles Scribner's, 1914), pp. 255, 191.

7. Edith Kilbuck to Carrie Weinland, November 1911, Weinland Collection, Huntington Library, San Marino, Calif., pp. 6–7.

8. Ibid., p. 6.

9. For books on missionaries in the Kuskokwim region, see Wendell H. Oswalt, *Mission of Change in Alaska: Eskimos and Moravians on the Kuskokwim* (San Marino, Calif.: Huntington Library, 1964) and Anna Buxbaum Schwalbe, *Dayspring on the Kuskokwim* Bethelehem, Pa.: Moravian Press, 1951). Various manuscripts written by the Moravian missionaries are in the William Weinland Collection at the Huntington Library.

10. Collier, *Eskimo Education*, pp. 11, 23, and 42.

11. See Sandra L. Myres, *Westering Women and the Frontier Experience, 1800–1915* (Albuquerque: University of New Mexico Press, 1982), pp. 12–36.

12. Louise Bogan, "Woman," in *Poems and New Poems* (New York: Charles Scribner's, 1941), p. 19.

13. Ted. C. Hinckley, *The Americanization of Alaska, 1867–1879* (Palo Alto, Calif.: Pacific Books, 1972), p. 203.

Life in Alaska

1. John Henry Kilbuck (1861–1922), a member of the Delaware Indian tribe, was born on a reservation in Kansas and educated in Moravian schools. He married Edith Romig of Kansas in 1885 and together they went to Bethel, Alaska, as Moravian missionaries. He taught in the village school at Akiak the year before May went there. He was Alaska's western district superintendent of education for the U.S. government from 1914 to 1918. John Kilbuck has become a legendary figure in Alaska; the Kilbuck mountain range south of Akiak is named for him.

2. The *Victoria* was a full-time Alaska liner from 1908 to 1954. Her best-known captain was John O'Brien (1848–1931), who was born in Cork, Ireland, and was famous for bringing the *Victoria* safely through any weather.

3. The Alaska Commercial Company had dominated trade and transportation in Alaska from the time it had bought out the Russian Trading Company there in 1868. In 1911, because of emerging competition, Alaska Commercial merged with its competitors to form two companies: The Northern Navigation Company, for transportation and shipping, and the Northern Commercial Company, for mercantile trade. The dominance of these two companies caused frequent complaints of economic monopoly in Alaska. The *Sarah* was one of the Northern Commercial Company's riverboats. See L. D. Kitchener,

Flag over the North: The Story of the Northern Commercial Company (Seattle: Superior Publishing Company, 1954).

4. Oscar Samuelson was a mail carrier in Alaska for many years. He later founded Oscarville, a village south of Bethel, which now has a population of about fifty people.

5. The portage was between the Yukon and Kuskokwim rivers at their closest point, a distance of about twenty-five miles. It was a region of tundra streams and lakes to be navigated and swampy passages to be crossed on foot.

Alaska literature includes at least two other accounts of crossing this portage. Anna Buxbaum Schwalbe, in *Dayspring on the Kuskokwim,* gives a less enthusiastic account than May Wynne's. Schwalbe writes of a trip made at an earlier date and without as competent a guide: "The portage, or low watershed, if it may be so called, is made up of winding, sluggish tundra streams, meandering through many miles to accomplish one. There are large lakes and there are pools of brackish water amid swampy stretches of "niggerheads" [hummocks or tussocks of vegetation]. These last must be crossed on foot. The traveler tries for sure footing but usually sinks ankle deep while the gases from the marsh bubble up at every step. Over these places, too, the boats must be dragged or carried. Millions of mosquitoes make the hours a torture. . . . Recrossing the portage was an ordeal that tried the strength of everyone. Fortunately the two missionaries had strength and endurance. The natives, while not so strong were their equals in holding out. Surefooted and conserving their energy, they could shoulder a hundred pound sack of flour, and slipping about among the niggerheads or slipping deep in the ooze, they went on and on and on. At the portages proper, the boats had to be unloaded and everything carried across. While they were crossing the largest lake, the wind blew up and their boats were in danger of capsizing. But at last they reached the Kuskokwim." Anna Buxbaum Schwalbe, *Dayspring on the Kuskokwim* (Bethlehem, Pa.: Moravian Press, 1951), pp. 80–81.

Another description of the portage is given by Hrdlička Aleš in *Alaska Diary, 1926–1931* (Lancaster, Pa.: Jacques Cattell, 1943). Making the journey in 1929, he found more amenities than did May Wynne and her companions. There was a roadhouse where travelers spent the night at the beginning of the first stretch to be crossed on foot and also a span of track and a manually operated car for transporting boats, baggage, and tents across land. However, Aleš made his journey in May, before the ice was all out of the water, and his story is one of tedious delays while waiting to maneuver his boat around the ice that still blocked parts of the river.

6. Lulu Evans was a government nurse at Akiak from 1916 to 1924 and at Bethel after 1924. In 1918 she married Jack Heron, the United States commissioner stationed at Bethel. He is mentioned by May in chapter 7. In 1935, Mrs. Heron wrote a report of her nursing activities at Akiak and Bethel for a study of the Alaska native population: H. Dewey Anderson and Walter Ells, *Alaska Natives: A Survey of Their Sociological and Educational Status* (Palo Alto: Stanford University Press, 1935), p. 407. The first paragraph of her account reads as follows: "In October 1916, the nurse arrived at Akiak on the Kuskokwim to pioneer in health work in this locality. There had been neither doctor nor nurse since Dr. Romig left Bethel in 1903. The month of October 1916, 136 patients were treated in Akiak, 166 in Bethel, 79 in Quichluk. Transportation for the nurse was furnished by boat, and outboard motors often failed to work. There was no doctor nearer than Nulato on the Yukon, and his advice as he met the nurse at midnight on the way down the river was, "Little woman, don't work too hard, do your best, and when you fail, remember that you are not God." [The doctor was Frank Lamb, then stationed at Nulato.] This comforted her as she stood by badly burned patients and pneumonia victims by the dozen that year, realizing that there was neither telephone, telegraph, nor radio to bring instructions to her about her patients. The work of 1916–17, when not treating tuberculosis, was entirely emergency first aid. In 1924 the appointment to Bethel as traveling nurse was made. Headquarters were established at Bethel, a unit by itself, independent of the hospital, to attempt the improvement of the sanitary and health conditions in that locality."

7. The name of the chief was Kawagaleg. This was the name he was called by the Moravian missionaries. The correct Yupik spelling was *Kavarliag*. He was chief of the village and the Moravian "helper," or minister, of the Akiak church.

8. Mrs. Omen was probably Mrs. Herman Omen, a nurse at the Akiak hospital in 1918. Her husband had a claim at Canyon Creek.

9. Joe Venus had come to Alaska at the time of the 1890s gold rush and by 1916 had made his way down to the Kuskokwim, where he worked a claim at Canyon Creek. George Olson and Karl Smith are not identifiable.

10. Reindeer and reindeer camps were not a part of the traditional native economy in Alaska. They had been introduced into the country

by Dr. Sheldon Jackson, an early Presbyterian missionary in Alaska who later lobbied in Washington for Eskimo interests, as he perceived them. He believed the animals would provide a valuable addition to the food supply, a means of transportation, and a source of skins for clothing, tents, bedding, and other items, as they did for certain groups of Arctic Siberian Eskimos. He imported sixteen reindeer into Alaska in 1891 as an experiment, and the following year Congress appropriated six thousand dollars to import a large number of reindeer from Siberia. At the time of the reindeer fair described, the industry was growing and flourishing and seemed to show that Jackson's hopes were well founded. After World War I, the reindeer industry in Alaska declined for various reasons, including lack of pasturage, attacks by wolves and other predators, the coming of air travel (which relieved winter food shortages), and the disinclination of the Eskimos to live away from their communities.

11. The deer May saw were probably those of a composite herd belonging to Eskimo herders and apprentices, Lapps, the Moravian mission, and the U.S. government. Ownership was indicated by notches in the reindeers' ears.

12. Raising a garden was one of May's duties as a teacher in an Alaskan native school. The governor's report on Alaskan schools in 1917 makes the following statement: "Agriculture is being developed through school gardens with very gratifying results. These school gardens may be found in almost every section of Alaska, and through this agency not only the interest of the younger generation is being stimulated but that of the entire village. . . . By a large production of vegetables and the storage of large quantities of dried fish, canned berries and other local products, the natives can live almost independently of outside supplies" (*Report of the Governor of Alaska* [Washington: U.S. Government Printing Office, 1917], p. 17).

13. John Felder and George Smith (mentioned in the following paragraph) were partners in the Felder-Galen Company at Akiak.